*There's More to Retirement
Than Driving Your Spouse*

# CRAZY

# There's More to Retirement Than Driving Your Spouse

# CRAZY

BY JOHN E. LEVEE

CWS President,
Advanced Wealth Strategies Group

Printed in the United States of America

Library of Congress Control Number: 2017954234

ISBN Paperback: 978-1-947368-33-0
ISBN eBook: 978-1-947368-34-7

Interior Design: Ghislain Viau

*I want to thank God for showing me my calling. It is wonderful to not have a job. It is even more wonderful to be able to work with and assist fantastic families. I thank everyone who has allowed us to be of service.*

*I would like to dedicate this book to my fantastic wife Laurie.*

*She is the one who convinced me we could do special things during our lifetime. She was right. We have been Blessed in so many amazing ways. She believed in me before I believed in myself, and she has always been there for me, all of our sons, and our six grandchildren.*

# Disclosures

This is neither an offer to sell nor a solicitation of an offer to buy securities. Any information contained in this book should not be used in making investment decisions. Investors should carefully consider the investment objectives, risks, charges, and expenses associated with any investment. Past performance is not indicative of future results. All investments involve a certain degree of risk. Opinions expressed are subject to change without notice.

Investing in alternative investments may not be suitable for all investors and may involve significant risks. These risks may include, but are not limited to, lack of liquidity, loss of principal, limited transferability, conflicts of interest and real estate fluctuations based upon a number of factors, which may include changes in interest rates, laws, operating expenses, insurance costs and tenant turnover. Investors should also understand all fees associated with a particular investment and how those fees could affect the overall performance of the investment. Neither Advanced Wealth Strategies Group, Animas Capital Management LTD , Advanced Capital Management, John Levee, IAN nor DFPG provide tax or legal advice, as such advice can only be provided by a qualified tax or legal professional, who all investors should consult prior to making any investment decisions.

Advanced Wealth Strategies Group and Animas Capital Management are branch offices of DFPG Investments, Inc. Securities offered through DFPG Investments, Inc. Member FINRA/SIPC. Investment Advisory Services offered through Integrated Advisors Network, LLC (IAN), a Registered Investment Advisor. DFPG Investments, Inc. and Integrated Advisors Network, LLC are not affiliated.

# Contents

# Foreword

AUTUMN MAKES ME FEEL MY AGE. LAST SATURDAY WAS cool and misty – the sort of September afternoon they tell stories about – and I spent it high in the forest canopy, a sloping view of the cloud-strewn mountain-side stretched out before me, accompanied only by my son and my bow. Hunting elk with a bow always stirs my competitive spirit, the side of me that aches for challenge and discovery. Our elk call sounded through the quiet of the forest, and we settled in to wait.

For me, the time feels heavy. It's a blessing, this time spent away from the hurly-burly of city life, but it didn't come out of nowhere. Life changes quickly and sometimes without warning, rocketing down a path marked as much by blind curves and steep hills as by inspiring vistas and flower-strewn scenery. I know that the choices I make every day – and the choices I made in my youth – have all contributed to the time I can take away from the office. The time I can now spend with my family, in the gentle silence of nature. The peace of these woods, the release of the tension I carry from day to day, is my reward for my life's work.

That's why working with a financial planner is so important. That's why having a plan in place is so crucial. Life is hard to predict. None of us can know what awaits us, and that uncertainty – that knowledge that danger could lurk around the next bend in the road – that's what keeps me up at night. Having a plan in place lets me sleep easy. It gives me the peace of mind I need to believe that no matter what happens, my family and I will be okay.

That peace of mind is worth everything. It's worth the work and the research and the time that make a financial plan truly viable. It's worth taking action – doing something is always better than doing nothing.

A good financial plan doesn't just fall fully-formed from the heavens. Today's economy is not the concrete foundation we'd all like it to be. Fluctuations in the market combined with ever-shifting regulations result in an economic reality that only a fool would rely on. Your financial plan cannot be written in stone. When the market changes, your financial plan should be able to change too, and quickly. It needs to be agile and flexible enough to account for all these twists in the road.

And, like any good vehicle, your financial plan will need regular maintenance. It will need to be monitored on a regular basis. It will need to make sense to everyone involved – husband, wife, advisor – everyone affected by its creation should know how it works and what it's meant to do. Building a financial plan is not a simple process of setting goals. We all understand that setting goals is important, but it alone won't be enough to truly set your mind at ease. You need to think about and prepare for the potential road-blocks and challenges that may bar your way. You need to have considered alternate routes and know ahead of time which sights you don't mind missing. You need to know what kind of life you're aiming for – not just what road markers of success you'll hit along the way.

Before we get too deep into the mechanics of figuring out what kind of financial plan is best for you, take a moment and really think about what success looks like for you. Is it the freedom to travel? A comfortable home? Is it, perhaps, a body of work you can keep adding to and taking pride in, far into your twilight years? (This last one is mine.) Knowing what you really want – not just believing that you have to work until you have *everything* – is essential to the peace of mind you'll find in a good financial plan. It lets you imagine what that success will feel like, and upon reaching it, it lets you feel the satisfaction that comes from life-long achievement.

A lot of that satisfaction comes from knowing you've made the right investment choices for your money. These choices are the heart of any financial plan, and they're determined entirely by your tolerance for risk. True risk tolerance is not something that can be measured by a simple twelve-page survey of your assets and debts. The question must be: how much risk do you feel comfortable taking on? You don't necessarily have to take on a huge amount of risk to see significant rewards. People will tell you that you do – that you can't see a 20% return on your investment without being willing to cope with a 40% loss when the market sours – but this simply isn't true. A good plan can potentially help you avoid the bad days and take advantage of the good ones. The only thing slowing down your return is your tolerance for risk.

So, how do you know how much risk you can tolerate? It sounds like a simple question, though you and I both know it's anything but. It's a question whose answer draws on your current finances – of course – though it also stems from a realistic estimate of how your money will grow. Financial planners the world over each have their own preferred way of working out this answer (though, if you meet with them and they don't help you through a risk assessment test, you're probably in the wrong place). We use a simple enough tool found right on our website – which lets our clients really dig down into how much they can invest, and what kind of risk levels they're willing to expose their investment to. It's just a few questions – not all that confusing, I swear – all designed to give our clients an at-a-glance understanding of their situation and help them work out how their current standing will affect their future. We like to give actual advice in person, and everyone's particular situation is different, but as a starting point, risk assessment tools work pretty well.

I believe that good plans are built by good teams, and that dedication results in quality work. I believe that the best plans are the ones that are custom built to fit your needs. The times have changed so much that if you're going to go through this important process of setting up a financial plan, working with an advisor you trust to respond competently to the market and to your needs is your wisest course of action. Naturally, I'm partial to our tools and our team, but there are many organizations to choose from. What's important is that you set up a financial plan *before* you need to fall back on it.

Life will speed along. Don't let it pass you by.

# CHAPTER ONE

# Let's Talk About Money

**B**Y NOW, WE'RE ALL FAMILIAR WITH HOW FINANCIAL planning works—in theory. I might know a little more than most; after more than 25 years in the industry and founding my own wealth strategies firms, I've seen my fair share of *Retirement Planning 101* manuals hit the shelves only to later be put to better use as doorstops. It's not that these manuals are the result of poor workmanship, or lack of knowledge, or some misguided desire to put you to sleep. It's just that, in order to disrupt the cycle of these one-size-fits-all planners, a.k.a. doorstops, a different approach is needed. And to formulate a different approach, you have to ask different questions.

The first question I'll always ask a client is strikingly different than the average financial advisor's opening volley. While another advisor might ask you boilerplate questions about what you think your own risk tolerance is (something, by the way, that is difficult for most people to accurately comprehend or describe and is usually not what their true tolerance really is), I'm curious about something else. Something more personal; something that really says a great deal about who you are and how you think, about where you're coming from. Something that helps me really get to know you. It's also one of my favorite questions to ask, because I get to hear some wonderful stories. I know we're only just getting acquainted, but you'll find out pretty quickly that I'm a fan of those kinds of questions.

So, right away I'm asking you to do a little pop quiz. There's no right or wrong answer, just *your* answer. The question I used to ask was: "What does money mean to you?" Ultimately, I came to the conclusion that this question was a bit too broad, so I narrowed it down. Instead, I'll start by asking you to **think about the very first thing you remember about money. What is that memory? And, to follow up, what does that memory—and the concept of money—mean to you?**

Everyone has a memory like this—maybe you remember collecting change on the side of the road at a rickety lemonade stand you made with a friend. Maybe your memory is a conversation you overheard between your mother and father, worrying about how they were going to pay the mortgage after your father's layoff. Maybe you remember the excitement that came with lifting your pillow the morning after you'd laid your first lost tooth underneath. Whatever the memory, I'm willing to bet that it speaks volumes about who you are now in relation to money. How you think of it. What it means to you.

I don't like to toss out questions that I'm too shy to answer, so I'll start. Hopefully it'll help jog your own memory, or memories, of the beginning of your relationship with money. My memory begins when I was a barefoot ten-year old, spending my summers working on my grandfather's ranch. I learned a lot from my grandfather about the power of prudent saving, and that lesson was seared into my brain when I almost lost my left ear because of a penny I saw on the ground at a shoe store. Here's the whole story:

Every summer of my childhood was spent with my siblings at my grandparents' house twenty-five miles north of Houston, Texas. It was real Texas backcountry, and I have no idea how my father convinced his parents to keep us all summer. I certainly could not get my parents to keep *my* four sons all summer. I hope my parents enjoyed the time off, because during those summers, *we* worked *our* butts off. I realize now it was a blessing, but at the time, I thought, "Gosh, weren't summers made for fun?"

Though my grandfather was retired at the time, he maintained five rental properties and was well known in the area as a man who could do just about anything, so he was frequently called upon to do various odd jobs. Whenever we worked with Grandpa, he would negotiate an hourly rate for my brother and I alongside his own hourly rate. Those hourly rates were typically twenty-five to fifty cents an hour for us kids, while my grandfather earned seventy-five cents to a dollar an hour. Now that's making money! We did all types of jobs, but one in particular stood out—a beautiful barbed wire fence we built for one of Grandpa's neighbors along their long driveway.

*[Side note: I learned a valuable lesson on this one: creosote posts will cause you great pain if you get the creosote on your neck. I remember at lunch Grandma put some sort of salve on it, and back to work we went.]*

When we finished that job, I remember being very proud of how good it looked. On both sides of the road the fence was nearly perfectly straight, and each wire was well-stretched and uniform. The fence was built using hand tools only, every posthole dug with manpower posthole diggers—no tractor with an auger for us. It was hard work for a little fella. That may be why to this day I am still proud of that fence.

That job taught me a valuable lesson; that hard work and doing the little things right without cutting corners or settling for less than your best is not acceptable. Those principals are still at work today in my personal and business lives. Grandpa was very strict, but also taught us lessons that would help us for the rest of our lives.

The most memorable (and least favorite) job with Grandpa was cleaning septic tanks with five gallon buckets. For those of you that don't know what a septic tank is let me explain. A septic tank is the main part of sewer systems in the country. It was back then a large (typically 300-500 gallons) concrete tank. It is virtually impossible to dip the liquids and solids out of the tank without getting some of the foul contents on you. (No wonder I now manage money for a living: it has a much nicer fragrance.) I remember complaining loudly and continuously until Grandpa imparted some of his wisdom by saying that "It won't hurt you, and it washes off with soap and water. Now get another bucket full so we can be done with it. We have other jobs to do!"

One of my favorite jobs as a youngster was working for my uncle, who lived near my grandfather and ran his own hay bailing business. There, I drove a tractor, pulling a rake to make neat piles of grass so my cousin could come along behind with the hay baler. Boy, did this beat shoveling or dipping sewage. To a young boy, driving the tractor was fun in and of itself. Getting paid to drive a tractor made it a total blast. I can't remember exactly how much I was paid; I'm pretty sure it was twenty-five or fifty cents an hour. I'll bet my aunt still has those records somewhere in her attic. My cousin, who was a year or so older, earned twice as much as me, and drove a beautiful new Massey Ferguson diesel tractor. I was pretty envious, but there wasn't much I could do; he was very close to the owners, after all.

Often, my siblings and I would spend Saturday night with my aunt and uncle after working in the hay fields all day. Sometimes, after a long day of working in the hot sun we would get to go swimming in the Rice Pond, a beautiful pond filled with clear, pure water. It had a monstrous pipe that shot water out several feet into the pond. No better way to relax and refresh after a hard day's work! One Saturday, it was determined that we would spend the night at my uncle's house rather than going back to my grandfather's. When the time came to go to church in the morning, I told my uncle that I didn't have any church shoes. Though we almost always went barefoot as kids, skipping church wasn't an option, so I had to go to church barefoot. I wanted to cry. I think I made up my mind then and there that would never happen to my kids.

I remember sitting there with my feet tucked under my chair, hoping and praying that nobody would notice. But they all did. I remember some of the other boys turned around and looked at me, barefoot and in my blue jeans and t-shirt, so embarrassed that I could feel a prickly heat burning all the way from my nose to my toes. The Baptist church that my aunt, uncle and cousins attended—particularly back then—was more formal than church today. You wouldn't show up in anything less than a suit, let alone without shoes to wear. And you can bet I didn't have a suit if I didn't have shoes. My uncle must have sensed my embarrassment and told my grandfather, which ultimately led to that fateful, painful trip to the shoe store in Houston not long after. But before I tell you about how I nearly lost an ear looking for shoes, I'd better describe Grandpa a little more.

Grandpa was a self-made man with a reputation for extreme frugality. It was said that he could squeeze a buffalo head nickel so hard the buffalo would appear on both sides. Though in his fifties, Grandpa still had the very first dollar he ever earned. He was a retired sheet metal worker, but remained active by maintaining his rental properties or doing odd jobs six days a week—some heckuva retirement! On Sunday, he would sit on a swing outside the breezeway and read the newspaper from cover to cover. We mowed the yard. God and Grandpa could rest on the Sabbath, but not the grandkids! Grandpa's education was cut short in the ninth grade, which is when he went to work and saved and saved and saved and saved. Even though he was retired, he maintained his sheet metal business, which was located on one of his rental properties. He was able to bend and shape huge pieces of stainless steel into a beautiful table and sink for one of his friends, all done without written instructions or illustrations. He was exactly the type of person who made this country great. My grandparents practiced what they preached, and I am thankful for the time I spent with them.

Now, back to the barefoot story. Grandpa took me to a shoe store in Houston, and as we were walking along, I spotted a penny on the sidewalk near the shop entrance. There was a bubble gum machine right inside the door of the shoe store, and as I picked up the penny, temptation got the best of me! Here's where it gets painful. Grandpa saw me grab the penny and run that shiny bit of copper into the bubblegum machine, but he didn't cheer my good fortune. He didn't watch the big pink ball roll down the chute and into my palm. He headed straight for my ear, clamping down on it with his fist, pulling me away from my folly. "You don't waste money on *bubblegum*," he growled me as I rubbed my raw, red ear. "You get a penny, you *save* it."

Lesson learned.

My own father was Grandpa's eldest son, and his polar opposite—spending everything that he earned. We never had a bad life—though it was tough at times—but I guess his own relationship and psychological makeup kept him from managing money properly and saving for retirement. I suppose he didn't see the point in keeping a rainy day fund. He thought he could fiddle until the day he died. Mission accomplished.

My dad was one of the first entrepreneurs I knew. He was always looking for a new way to make money—anything to stay away from the 9-to-5 grind. I must have inherited that gene from him, since I too have been a business owner for the majority of my working life. And it wasn't that he was incapable: at various points in his career, my dad was a salvage diver and a deer releaser, and his other numerous jobs were no less exciting. For the most part we had a pretty darn good life, even though my father's search for his calling sometimes left us short on money. He started a meat market that lasted only a year. When it closed, we kept the leftover meats, and my lunches for the rest of the school year consisted of salami sandwiches. I haven't eaten salami since!

I guess he rebelled against his father, who saved everything, squirreling away $3,000 in his sock drawer at a time before making a trip to the bank in Houston, twenty miles away. Before going to the bank Grandpa would make us sit at the kitchen table and count out each dollar, all *three thousand* of them while he gave us a speech about the importance of saving. Grandpa rarely ventured into Houston, and it meant taking a big trip.

Yet Grandpa had suffered the journey to the shoe store because he wouldn't let me attend church barefoot. Forget about the value of a dollar, my grandfather was keenly aware of the value of every single cent.

This experience stuck with me not only because I almost lost an ear, but because it taught me that people view money in very different ways and that those views have a profound effect on their lives. On the one hand, I had a grandfather who saved everything, eschewing fun, travel, and amusement, and then on the other, my father, who made a lot of money but had a hard time hanging onto it, choosing fun over prudence.

It's not my place to sit in judgement over my father and grandfather's different approaches to money, but I do know that the Bible tells us, "It is a wise man that leaves an inheritance to his son." (Proverbs 13:22). Since I believe in the Bible, I suppose I should think my father unwise. Yet he taught me to be honest, to have a solid work ethic, and to love people.

I keenly feel the tug of responsibility – I am obligated to leave something to my sons. I am obligated to spend the rest of my life helping people manage their money wisely so as to realize their financial goals. As the son of a man who died without much to his name and who now makes a living assisting others in their money-managing endeavors, I know how much my story tells you about me and my relationship with money.

I will do everything in my power to help families successfully navigate the seas of investment strategies that most people will never understand. My desire to help people is insatiable! The story of my grandfather and my sore ear is more than a revelation of some of my family's work ethic and money dynamics; it also distills important parts of my financial philosophy.

The same can be said for the stories my clients tell me. They come into my office and we begin our conversation with their first memories of money. I work with people from all walks of life, folks who come to me from technology, government, and small businesses. Some of my clients were born with a silver spoon in their mouths, and some of them, like me, started with nothing and had to claw their way up.

I remember one client talking about growing up in poverty and, as a child, not having money to clean the few garments she had. She felt filthy and ashamed, coming to school in clothes that she'd worn all week. It profoundly affected her self-esteem. She knew that, no matter what, she didn't want her children to go through what she had endured. It put my story about going to church barefoot to shame. "We were very, very poor," she told me, not mincing words, tears forming in her eyes. "And I never want to be like that again. Ever."

Without going into complicated theories about asset allocation, without talking about risk tolerance or time horizons, I was able to get a picture of this woman—a very raw, intimate portrait. I learned that she's conservative, a big-time saver, like my grandpa. I saw that she would be concerned with making sure that her money didn't run out in her retirement years. I saw that she would want to spend a great deal of time on legacy planning, on making sure that her children never had to suffer like she had. She saw life stretching out in front of her and wanted to live it to the best of her ability without ever again having to worry about putting food on the table or about her children going to bed hungry.

That's pretty powerful. Starting with a personal narrative makes it easier for me and my team to provide useful, custom-crafted financial advice that goes beyond being an asset allocator, money manager, or financial planner. It's easier to grasp the whole person, the whole picture—did this person come from a wealthy family and receive adequate training on managing large sums of money? Did this person come up from nothing, having to scratch together scraps and pennies to survive? No two clients are the same, and no two plans are the same. It's amazing how much we can find out just by asking the right questions.

Another example of one of these questions is: **If you're planning to retire, in a perfect world, what does retirement look like to you?** I'll go first, again, although it might not be so helpful when you hear the answer—it's the truth! I don't personally feel the need to retire; I love what I do, and my perfect "retirement" would actually entail, as long as my good health allows, me being able to continue working. It's by no means mandatory that you retire when you're sixty-five. Plenty of people are living longer and working longer, and, due to the mounting problems with Social Security, this is a trend that is only going to grow.

The key is that you should be able to use your retirement years for something you *want* to do—again, in your perfect world. Unlike my father, who *had* to work until he died at age seventy-nine and was unable to leave any assets behind, I want to keep working because I *enjoy* working. I'm sixty-five years old, and you'd better believe I'm setting up a business succession plan—my son, Derek, is a portfolio manager—so he and my top Round Rock advisor Chris will be able to take care of our clients when I'm gone. I'm spending these years exactly the way I want to—by helping protect as many people as humanly possible from ending up like my dad.

All of our clients know we utilize a team approach, so they can rest easy knowing there will always be someone available to take care of them. We train and promote from within so that all of our staff is trained in our special way of treating and taking care of clients. Clients are not just a number in our offices. I have told most of our clients that my perfect death would occur during a client meeting and that Derek or Chris would just move me over to the side of the conference room and then continue and finish their review. Crazy? Maybe. But it's true. When you truly love what you do, you don't have a job, you've got something you were meant to do.

Your answer might be different. You might want to travel the globe. You might want to settle down in one place and spend time with your grandchildren. You might want to volunteer for your favorite charity, or take up a new hobby. No matter what your answer is, the answers that this question reveals can become the basis for our planning. We have clients that do everything from traveling the globe, volunteering at hospitals or shelters, making deliveries for Meals on Wheels, and building homes across the globe with Habitat for Humanity. I appreciate how our clients are using their retirement to better the lives of their fellow man. I hope and pray that we are doing the same.

The third question will likely relate to their investment experience. What type of investing have clients done in the past, and if there are any investments they are totally opposed to. Have they used an advisor before? If so, how was that experience? It's not important to me that you've had any experience at all (that's what I'm here for!), but it is important that I have an idea of what those experiences might be and of what ideas and concerns you might have regarding investing, regardless of whether or not you've dabbled in the past. I want to get at the root of what you're looking for from our financial relationship. What have you done in the past that you might be uncomfortable with now? What makes you feel that way? Are there types of investments that you don't understand? If there are, those are the things we need to discuss.

While a typical investment planning firm may make these first conversations all about the *numbers*, I'm interested in your *feelings*. Have you experienced major market downturns? If so, how did that make you feel, and what were you invested in during those times? Do you remember 2008 and 2009? How did you feel when you saw your 401(k) become a 201(k)—or worse? Many clients who came to us after the damage had been done said it got so bad they couldn't even stand to open their quarterly statements. What did the advisor you were working with tell you? How did that make you feel? Were you satisfied with their explanations? I'm interested in what's important to you and what makes you tick, because then, and only then, will I be able to come up with a plan that's right for you.

So, what do our plans end up looking like? Rather than running the risk of becoming a broken record—or one of those doorstops I was worried about earlier—I can give you a peek into the process, with the caveat that retirement planning looks different for everyone. Typically, after asking some of these time-tested questions, we are able to understand what our clients' needs are for the short-, intermediate-, and long-term. We actively manage funds using a simple strategy that we lay out for our clients on a four-page spreadsheet that shows our clients where they are and where they hope to be. We meet with our clients quarterly, making recommendations and involving them in the process, making changes as needed when life throws its inevitable curveballs. We show our clients how long we see their portfolio lasting. We talk about the three phases of retirement: "go time," when they are ready and able to travel; "go slow" time, when they start to settle down a little more; and the "no go" time, which is when they need to be in a stable place receiving adequate care in their twilight years.

All of this is shaped by industry best practices, and cutting edge research tools coupled with many years of experience under fire. Any financial advisor worth their salt would or should be able to say that. What sets us apart? I'd like to think it's those questions we ask, the real ones, the ones that let us get down to brass tacks without wasting any of our clients' valuable "go time." The bottom line doesn't get illuminated when you throw a thick pile of graphs and scenarios across the table. The bottom line doesn't become clear when you talk about unrealistic scenarios and boilerplate advice. The real bottom line rests in the answer to one of my other favorite questions: **What do you want to do with your life?**

No matter what your answer is, it should be true, it should be you, and it should be something your financial advisor should be able to help you achieve. Because you've got to fill those 18 hours of your day with something other than ***driving your spouse crazy***. You've got to start talking about retirement not as Return on Investment (ROI), but Return on Life (ROL).

What the heck is Return on Life? I'm glad you asked. Return on Life is enjoying your retired life to its fullest, doing and accomplishing all you dreamed of as you prepared for retirement without fear and daily concern. It is enjoying the path to retirement without giving up everything else to accomplish your goals.

Is this really possible? Absolutely.

Ready? Okay. Now we're talking.

## The Garden of Eden

A financial advisor, an engineer, and a doctor are arguing over which profession is the oldest.

The doctor says, "Just look at Genesis! When God removes Adam's rib to make Eve, that's a surgical procedure."

The engineer replies, "In the very first line of the Bible, it says that there was chaos, and then God created the Earth. That's an engineering task,"

Then the financial advisor says, "Who do you think created all of the chaos?"

# CHAPTER TWO

# If You Don't Want to Run Out of Money, Know What to Ask

THERE ARE NO GUARANTEES IN FINANCE, EVEN IF YOU'RE making use of the help of qualified professionals. Any financial advisor worth his salt will tell you that there's no magic formula to unlocking the timing and fluctuations of the markets. That being said, there are some things that, throughout my years of experience, I've come to accept as what amounts to a working philosophy for my firm. While the first part of our initial meeting with clients revolves around asking them the questions that we explored in the first chapter, we also cover questions that they should be asking us—or any financial advisor they employ, for that matter. Here are the questions you, the client, should always ask your financial advisor:

## Question #1: What's your strategy for the next bear market?

It's easy to get amped up on the idea of bull markets. We've seen some great ones, and we'll continue to see periods of growth.

But having a reasonable and realistic view means understanding that there's going to be bad mixed with the good. We know from past history that bear markets will happen. Exactly when the next one will come along is anybody's guess, but they will come. Most would agree that it is not terribly hard to make money during raging bull markets. After all, doesn't a rising tide raise all boats? As super investor Warren Buffet famously said in a letter to shareholders in 2001: **"After all, you only find out who is swimming naked when the tide goes out."**[1]

And trust me, some of these bear markets can get pretty bad. When you're sitting down with your financial advisor, you'll need to ask them what their strategy will be when it comes to dealing with these bear markets.

We tell our clients that, for our part, we can only prepare them for the ***certainty of uncertainty***. That may seem a little paradoxical, but it's just what you want to hear from a good financial advisor. It means that we acknowledge the fear and uncertainty that clients face in any market; there's a lot of uncertainty out there in the world! What's going to happen with Russia and the Ukraine? How about Greece or Spain? How will those geo-political situations affect the European markets? What will turmoil in the Middle East do to oil prices, and how does that affect the dollar? Will our next president be Democrat or Republican? How will

---

1 Ro, Sam. "Warren Buffett's 23 Most Brilliant Insights About Investing." Business Insider. August 31, 2014. Accessed February 11, 2016. http://www.businessinsider.com/warren-buffetts-investing-quotes-2014-8?op=1#ixzz3W5gSoyAK.

that affect the markets? A modern man's list of worries goes on and on. A good financial advisor embraces the uncertainty by monitoring his clients' investments on a *daily* basis. That's what we do: constantly shifting conditions require constant vigilance and possible adjustments. There are always going to be questions and concerns. Remember—we live in an imperfect world, run by imperfect people, so there are always going to be problems. We take the emotions out of investing. We can do that. Most clients cannot!

## Question #2: Is your strategy a buy and hold strategy?

When interviewing a financial advisor, you want to take care to understand the strategies they employ, and get to the bottom of why they subscribe to those strategies. Just because you've hired someone to help you on your financial journey doesn't excuse you from having to do some heavy lifting of your own! No one cares more about your money than you do, so make your time count. Don't be afraid to ask these questions, and to question assumptions.

While many advisors will use a buy and hold strategy, I don't fall into that camp. We'll explore this in depth later in the book, but for starters, the buy and hold strategy may not always be the most appropriate way to deal with the uncertainty of the markets. It's certainly one of the ways, but not the *only* way. When you buy and hold, you run the risk of riding a market trend downward. This isn't such a big deal for a twenty-something who has his earning years ahead of him, but for someone in or approaching retirement, it can be catastrophic. While markets do bounce back, it can take many years to recoup those losses. Our philosophy is that missing the worst days is far more important than catching all of the good days.

No one can miss all of the bad days and no matter what strategy you implement, the risk of loss is real. But if you can miss a good number of those bad days, there is a chance that you can spare yourself the agony of riding a bear market all the way to the bottom. No, I'm not talking about timing the market. We learned a long time ago that risk management was crucial and started following Warren Buffet's mentor's advice. As you can see from the quote below, Mr. Graham was more concerned about risk than returns.

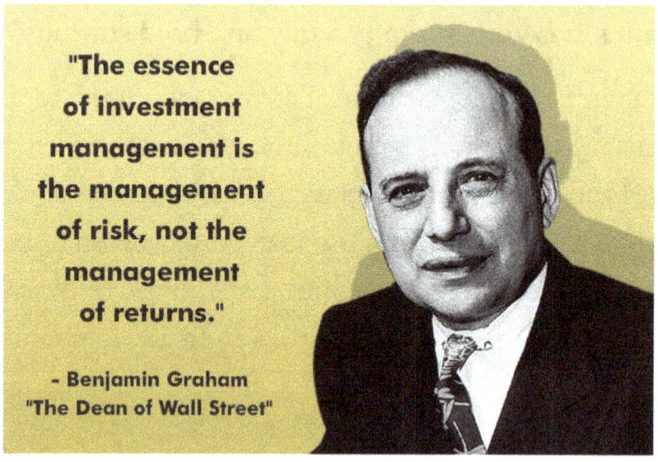


So, how exactly do we do that? The answer is proper—and I mean *proper*—diversification. What is proper diversification? How about owning stocks, bonds and cash? Is that proper diversification? Owning large-cap, mid-cap and small cap stocks – is that proper diversification? All of the above is true to some degree, but the reality is still more complicated. It's hard for the layperson to create and build a truly diversified portfolio because they may not be able to get certain products or strategies on their own. They may not have access to some of the alternative investments, especially the alternative investments that we'll get to in the next question.

## Question #3: Do you use alternative investments? If so, what kind?

When you buy and hold, you are using a strictly long-term strategy where you've found some decent stocks and mutual funds, and you've spread your money across the stock market and into small caps, medium caps, and large caps. When the market goes down, you don't panic, you just hold on to what you've got and ride it out. You think your eggs aren't all in one basket—that you're all over the market—so you're going to be safe.  Right?

We say: "wrong!" While it's a great idea to be diversified, being diversified doesn't just mean buying a variety of stocks. You have to diversify your products.

In our office we combat this issue by using alternatives for up to 25 percent of our client portfolios—meaning we've got clients employing other areas of the economy, such as real estate and other types of investments, which are less correlated to the stock market. This helps us to potentially reduce the volatility of our client accounts when a bear market hits and stocks plummet. This is a strategy employed by the University of Texas endowment fund, which, according to a Bloomberg Business article, at the time of publication, recently passed Yale University as the second largest endowment fund at $25.4 billion[2].

Why do we even talk about endowment funds? Endowment funds have figured out that there is more to investing than just the stock market. Those folks strategically re-allocated a portion of the

---

2 http://www.bloomberg.com/news/articles/2015-01-29/university-of-texas-endowment-tops-25-billion-surpassing-yale

university's assets into alternatives. We aren't large enough to have the versatility of these mega-wealthy university endowment funds, but we've created a **Family Endowment Model** for our clients to follow, which is largely inspired by the varied and strategic models used by Harvard University or the University of Texas. By mixing traditional investments with alternative investments, these investments add diversity to your portfolio. Remember, in our opinion – and that of many other highly respected investors and money managers – risk *must* be managed.

## Question #4: What about budgeting? Will we talk about this?

If the answer to this question is "No," or "We don't need to," stop right there, do not pass go, do not let them collect your money! If you don't want to run out of money in retirement, you'll need a clear and consistent budget. Your financial advisor should run projections on retirement income, keeping an eye on where that income comes from, if it's tax efficient, and how that income may be protected from downside volatility. With your earning years largely behind you, you can't be flying by the seat of your pants.

A good financial advisor will help you come up with a budget that covers your needs while keeping you covered. By using conservative growth rates, your financial advisor should be able to demonstrate what your retirement income can realistically look like each year. If you're preparing to retire and it seems as though your retirement income can't cover your expenses, your financial advisor should be able to help you get a clear picture of what kind of cushion you'll need to build up, how long you should continue to work, and so forth. If they present a model where your money is growing at something over 5% a year in retirement, then that's another red flag – run the other way! Our philosophy is to pray for the best, but prepare for the worst. You should look at the best and worst case scenarios. After all, it is your life.

## Question #5: Who will be minding my money? Do you utilize a team approach, or an individual approach?

Many people want to have a personal, one-on-one relationship with their financial advisor. That shouldn't come at the expense of the benefits of a team approach, however. If your financial advisor runs a one-man shop, who is minding the store when he's out on a three-week vacation, or if he gets sick and can't return emails? Planning for retirement—and the narrow margin of error for living on a fixed retirement income—is simply too critical to trust to an overloaded, overworked person who also has to worry about paperwork and answering phones.

It's too critical to trust to unqualified office staffers who may be the only ones minding the store when their boss is away. By utilizing a team approach, we make sure that a qualified, trained, licensed professional is always available for our clients, as well as a trained support staff available to assist whenever necessary. Our clients know as well as I do that I have a finite time on this earth. Neither you nor I are guaranteed another breath. Therefore, my clients are utilizing the benefits of the company, not the benefits of John Levee. They know that if I do (literally) run out of breath, the firm has other trained professionals (with the proper education, training, and credentials) who can help them continue with their retirement goals.

## Question #6: How much experience does your team have?

You'll want a collective experience level represented by decades rather than single digits. This isn't to say that advisors new to the field aren't worth their weight, but by having a team of qualified professionals mentoring the newer advisors, there is a good chance that the continuity of good work that has been built up over generations is getting passed down along with the client list. One of the worst things I can imagine is to have your hard earned assets managed by someone who is inexperienced and is earning as he or she is learning.

## Question #7: Who's vouching for the firm's work in its advertisements? Who represents the public face of the firm?

This is a pretty specific question, but we've included it because all too often we'll see clients get wowed by celebrities like movie stars and political figures endorsing a financial institution on television commercials. Just like when a celebrity endorses a clothing line or product, that celebrity has most likely been *paid* to say kind words about that product. I always wonder if they are putting their trust in the company they are advertising or if they would just like you to invest so that they can get their paycheck. Your retirement is far too important to trust to a firm that would attempt to have you believe the word of an actor when it comes to their end product. Beware the faces on the squawk box and in financial publications. Just because they appear on television or write for a major magazine does not mean they are good investment managers. I know of several such pundits who had terrible performance during the last bear market.

## Question #8: Do you use backup research firms? If so, which ones?

Although research firms cannot guarantee investment success, a good financial advisor will invest in firms that actively monitor the markets, providing in-depth and instantaneous research as advisors continue to shape and re-shape strategies for clients in changing and uncertain markets. Ask your advisor which research firms he uses, and how long those firms have been in the industry. Having backup research firms in the mix can help a well-developed, well-founded strategy. It's also important that these firms are *independent*, and have no stake in the products that they are reviewing or recommending.

## 😄 *Joke Time* 😄

## The Road to Riches

A young man asked a financial advisor how he made his money.

The financial advisor touched his collar and said, "It was the financial crash of 2009. One of the worst bear markets I've ever seen."

"People were scrambling for answers. At first, I billed clients 100 dollars an hour."

"The next month, I raised my rates to 200 dollars an hour."

"Then my wife's father died and left us 12 million dollars."

# CHAPTER THREE

# Just Ride Out the Storm?
# Like Hell!

As YOU LEARNED IN THE LAST CHAPTER, ONE OF THE most important questions to ask your advisor is: *What's your strategy?* It bears repeating—if your guy tells you that his strategy is buy and hold, you should head for the hills. My firm hasn't subscribed to that view for over twenty years. Although there are no guarantees in finance or in life, I can certainly try to share with you what I've learned from experience in the hopes that you'll be able to avoid some of those pitfalls.

In my opinion, the buy and hold strategy of today is an outmoded strategy, based in part on modern portfolio theory (MPT), which stretches back to the 1930s. Proponents of MPT will say that they've got eighty-odd years of history on their side and that buying and holding is the only way to ensure that you catch the high tides to balance out the low ones that temporarily leave you stranded. But in my view, you wouldn't allow yourself to receive outdated medical treatment, so why are you allowing yourself to receive outdated financial advice?

The reason that buy and hold is inefficient isn't so much its age, although that has something to do with it. While historical precedent is useful in theory, it's not necessarily applicable to today's reality. The same events that happened over the past eighty years are not going to happen in exactly the same way over the next eighty. Although history does repeat itself, it doesn't quite work like that in finance. Particularly since the recession of 2008, interventions by the government and the Federal Reserve—artificially inflating and depressing certain rates, buying bonds, bailing out the financial industry—have caused the stock market to behave in unnatural ways. Comparing the stock market of the present to the stock market of the past is an apples-and-oranges situation: it just doesn't match up.

Those with our thumbs on the pulse of the market have been forced to change our strategy as we've come to realize that the old buy and hold tactics won't work. We've looked at the trap that others are falling into as they continue to try the same old tricks, and we've worked to sidestep that by looking at other indicators. While some firms say that they've been able to keep up with changing market conditions by availing themselves of the latest technology, we've found that in and of itself, technology isn't enough to counteract the market forces at work today, either—the manipulation of the markets causes just as much trouble for computer programs as it does for us. Financial reports written with the past eighty years as a historical baseline give false signals to today's markets, and as result, investors relying solely on computer trading are forced into making and reversing decisions very quickly, trying to keep step with the market fluctuations responding to the latest Fed action, sometimes taking an equal number of steps forward and back. That's a dangerous little dance.

Another strategy that has been heavily misinterpreted in these uncertain times is diversification. While diversification is never a bad thing—there's a reason why the old adage about not having your eggs in the same basket sticks around, after all—diversification alone isn't enough to protect you in times of market downturn. Spreading your money across all the asset classes available (foreign and emerging markets, cash, bonds, etc.) doesn't necessarily mean that you'll do well on aggregate. These sectors don't always work in harmony with one another. For example, small and mid-caps underperformed in 2014. Foreign stocks also underperformed. The stocks that performed the best were large cap stocks. So although you may have been diversified between small and mid-caps, foreign and large caps, your portfolio would still underperform.

In our opinion, true diversification consists of much more than just owning stocks and bonds. It also should include assets not directly correlated to the stock market. There are a multitude of other investments available.

## How Our Strategy Differs

The first area that distinguishes our firm from those who employ buy-and-hold tactics is that we've appropriately adjusted the parameters of our research, as well as heavily invested in a dedicated firm to conduct our research in accordance with those parameters.[1]

Instead of falling behind ever-changing trends or attempting to time the market, we're *actively managing* our clients' funds. It's important to emphasize that this is different than timing the market, which is virtually impossible, and inefficient at best. For the layperson, that assessment would even be generous! There's simply no way to time the market. What we're doing is following trends on a more focused time horizon, rather than the longer-term trends that we followed in the past, since they aren't really applicable in this Wild West of an economy.

And we do believe things are only about to get wilder: the public has a false sense of security about the economic recovery, in part because of the government-induced stimulus measures. While there *has* been some recovery, it's been a slow one—all of the economic indicators show that it's been a long, uphill climb, except, perhaps, for the market itself, where we've basically had a five-year bull run-up, with a head-fake of sorts happening in 2011. During that time frame, we expected to see a major correction or two along the way. Letting yourself be lulled into a false sense of security by this slow recovery is one way in which investors may get hurt during the next bear market, which is coming, whether we want to believe it or not. And while a young person just entering their working life will likely be able to recover from those doldrums with relative ease,

---

1 Although no level of research and expertise can completely mitigate risk, good research can be valuable for representatives and their investors with a carefully selected suite of alternative investment solutions.

given the benefit of time, a client on the cusp of (or in the middle of) retirement cannot afford to take a 50 percent hit on his portfolio. If you're within five years of retirement when this happens, and if you're not prepared, you're going to be in serious trouble—and you'll definitely have to delay or postpone your retirement. When I say that this is serious business, trust me.

As I mentioned in the previous chapter, when searching for the right financial advisor, you should not only ask what the overall strategy for managing your money will be, but specifically find out if that advisor has a bear market strategy. If they do, have them show it to you, ask them what the strategy is, and what the details are. Ask them to show you what your portfolio would have looked like in 2008-2009, so that you can get a realistic idea of what you would be working with—and what you would have lost. All too often, even advisors have a short-term memory when it comes to the bear markets, selectively blotting out details they'd rather not remember. But putting your head in the sand when a predator is around doesn't mean you're not going to get eaten—the danger doesn't disappear when you stop paying attention to it. It only increases.

Apart from long-term memory loss, advisors can run into trouble when they don't have their clients' portfolios under active management. The good news is that if you do your due diligence and find a firm that is able to work in your best interest, you may have a better chance of navigating the changing dynamics of the market, rather than being caught unaware.

I know this from hard-won personal experience. In 2002, while visiting with family, an uncle approached me to ask for some financial advice. Our country was in the throes of a recession, the "tech bubble" had just burst, interest rates had risen and the stock market was continuing to drop. The S&P 500 had dropped 9.11 percent in 2000, 11.89 percent in 2001 and would drop 22.10 percent later in 2002. The mutual fund he was using mirrored the S&P 500, so I could understand his angst. He had all of his assets—his own retirement fund, his grandkids' college funds, everything he had—wrapped up in the same mutual fund. It was getting smoked!  I told him in no uncertain terms that he should get out of the market, but he was hesitant. "John, if I do that, I'll lose all my money," he said. "If I stay in, I won't really have lost anything. The market will come back and then I'll get it back."

"That is a mostly true statement," I told him. "Over time, the money does return. But I hope you don't need it during the time it takes to recover—because it could be years!"

I'm not sure why he didn't listen to me—I think he might have had a hard time picturing me as the financial advisor I am today. He'd always known me as a barefooted kid nicknamed "Bubba" who spent his summers running around on Grandpa's farm. I knew I hadn't gotten through to him, but I didn't push the issue; I felt that it was his place to make the decision. When his portfolio took a 22 percent hit in 2002 alone, I felt horrible that I hadn't sat him down and more clearly explained why I wanted him to get out. During those three years, he lost almost half of his wealth, and if he hadn't had the luxury of time to get it back, he and his family could have been in a world of hurt. In the business, we call it ugly math—when you go down 50 percent, you have to make a 100 percent gain just to call it even. Think about how long it might take to make a 100 percent gain in the stock market. Wouldn't it be terrible to suffer a loss like that right when you're about to retire? Avoiding those losses in the first place is the only way to stop that kind of bleeding, particularly when you're on a fixed income with limited or no earning potential to staunch the wound.

Part of why I'm writing this book for you right now is to keep that terrible future from happening to as many people as possible. Our clients' assets have been actively managed since 1993, with a focus on protecting the downside volatility. Research has shown that the market's worst days do more damage to the average portfolio than the market's best days can repair. For example, pretend that we've invested $1,000 in the stock market. A bad day comes along and the market loses 50 percent, taking our investment to $500. Then a good day arrives and the market gains 50 percent. But that only brings our investment back to $750. To really help us, good days would have to move the market upward much, much more than bad days move the market downward—and that's not how history says the market moves. When we discovered this, our asset management lives were changed forever and our focus turned immediately to a simple mantra: protect, protect, protect.[2]

Below, reprinted with the permission of the author (and to whom I again say a monstrous *Thank You,*) is an article written by Bob Brooks, author of the book *Deceptive Money* and host of the daily financial talk show, "The Prudent Money Show." The article

______

2 All investments involve a certain degree of risk.

is titled, "Missing the Worst Days in the Market Might Make You Rich,"[3] and it tackles this topic to a T.

## "Missing the Worst Days in the Market Might Make You Rich," by Bob Brooks.

Reprinted by permission of the author.

*John Bogle, founder of Vanguard Mutual Fund Company, says that market timing never works. Of course, any executive of a mutual fund company does not want investors moving money around. Besides his obvious bias, I don't think that he is entirely correct stating an absolute.*

*Market timing is a misunderstood concept when it comes to investing. The mutual fund industry defines market timing as a process of attempting to perfectly time the tops of markets (before a market declines) and perfectly time the bottom of stock market declines (before the stock market goes up).*

*In other words, an investor is trying to sell at the perfect time and buy at the perfect time. The mutual fund industry doesn't want you to time the market. Thus, they came up with a perfect example of why market timing is a disastrous strategy.*

*The basis of their argument is that if you try to time the market you might miss the best days of the month or year. If you miss those days when the market has big gains, then your overall investment return will really suffer. So they publish these studies.*

---

3 Brooks, B., 2016 (?), "Missing the Worst Days of the Market Might Make You Rich," prudentmoney.com. (unpublished)

*Barron's Magazine published an article that showed what an investor would have made if invested in the S&P 500 index from February 1966 through October 2001. During that 36-year period, an initial investment of $1,000 would be worth $11,710.*

*A study done by Birinyi Associates performed a complement study to the one in Barron's. They stated that if an investor missed the five best days every calendar year, the $1,000 would have shrunk to $150.*

*That is pretty convincing. An average investor would look at that statistic and conclude that market timing is a horrible strategy. Why would you want to try and pick when to be in the stock market and when to be out of the stock market? If you just missed a few good days, you might miss the entire opportunity.*

*I ran my own study. I wanted to know what would happen if you missed the worst months to be in the stock market. I took a look at the S&P 500 between January 1950 and December 2007.*

*If you invested $10,000 January 1950, it would have grown to $869,120 by December 2007.*

*If you missed the 30 best months, that $11,000 would have turned into $284,167. If you would have just stayed invested and not tried market timing, your $10,000 would have turned into $3,069,325. Instead, you tried to market time and ended up with only $35,404.*

*What if you would have missed the 30 worst months between January 1950 and December 2007?*

*If you missed the 30 worst months, your $1,000 would have turned into $9,509,094.*

*Which do you think is more important? Being in there for the gains or protecting yourself in the bad markets?*

*This isn't about market timing and trying to pick tops and bottoms of the market. This is about protecting your investments when stock market risk gets high. Remember you reduce risk as you reduce the amount of money invested in stocks.*

*When you experience excessive losses, it just takes so much time to gain back the loss.*

| Loss | percent Required to Break Even |
| --- | --- |
| -10 percent | +11 percent |
| -20 percent | +25 percent |
| -30 percent | +43 percent |
| -40 percent | +67 percent |
| -50 percent | +100 percent |
| -60 percent | +150 percent |
| -70 percent | +233 percent |

*If you were to lose -40 percent, it would require a return of 67 percent just to get back to even again. It would take a long time to achieve that return. This is why risk matters and having a risk strategy is extremely important.*

*Now obviously neither you or I are going to be able to look into the future and pick good and bad days in the market. This is just to illustrate the impact of loss on a portfolio. This is primarily directed towards investors who stay heavily invested in stocks. At some point you have to start taking profits and get your portfolio balanced and properly diversified. The problem is that most people are not properly diversified.*

The above article is for illustrative purposes only and past performance does not guarantee future results.

## 😄 *Joke Time* 😄

Albert Einstein goes to heaven and meets three other new guests. He asks the first guest, a physicist, his IQ.

"196, sir," says the first.

"Excellent," says Einstein. "I look forward to talking about my theory of relativity with you."

Einstein asks the same question to the second, a schoolteacher:

"150," says the second.

"Not bad," Einstein says. "We can discuss pressing problems of world justice and peace."

Einstein asks the third person the same question:

"75, sir," is the reply.

Einstein thinks for a minute, and then asks, "So, how do you think the economy will do next year?

# CHAPTER FOUR

# Why Our Plans Live, Breathe and Change with You

JUST AS MARKETS AND TRENDS CHANGE WITH THE global economic fluctuations, our clients' lives change, too. It would be foolish to think that you can write a financial plan, set it in stone, and toss it in a drawer somewhere to collect dust. Well, you *can* do that, but that doesn't mean you *should*. This is one of those red flags we've been talking about—if it seems like a financial advisor doesn't want to give you a living, breathing plan, you need to skedaddle, and fast.

Obviously, we do things a little differently. We know that life circumstances can change (for the better, the worse, or just take a new turn), and that's why we've always made it our practice to create plans that can keep up with those changes. And this means increasing our time commitment to our clients, making sure we meet quarterly (at least!) as opposed to annually or even semi-annually, keeping abreast of what's new with them.

So much can transpire in a twelve-month period that could affect a client's financial or estate planning—not to mention the fact that if you wait a year to talk to someone about something, no matter how important, it's not likely they'll remember to tell you everything that you need to know. We're talking family issues, divorces, big moves, long-term care issues, and more. These are all multi-faceted situations that can affect short- and long-term financial planning, goals in a variety of ways, and we want to know about all of them. On a personal level, we want to make sure we connect with our clients often so that we can be there for them during these times, too—we're providing a service, and part of that service entails figuring out how we can help when life throws a curveball, as it inevitably will.

Some of the concerns around meeting quarterly and keeping up with life changes are obviously financial, but some of our concerns are logistical in nature, and equally important. Beneficiary designations are one thing that can change throughout one's life, and it's crucial that these are updated in order to help ensure smooth passage of assets like retirement accounts or life insurance policies. When someone passes away unexpectedly—or neglects to update this information when dealing with a lengthy illness—it's another frustrating and unnecessary layer of trouble heaped on an already considerable pile. No matter how much we'd like to help, we are sometimes not authorized to make these changes, and so it then falls to the client—or the client's surviving relatives—to deal with the fallout. By meeting with our clients quarterly, we're able to keep a finger on the pulse of some of these changes, and are able to help steer them away from that frustration before it happens.

Quarterly meetings also insure that our clients become more invested in the process—they've got some skin in the game, so to speak. It's easy for them to forget about us, like you might forget about a gym membership or a promise to eat healthy. If we're in regular contact with each other, it brings the whole situation in focus. As clients creep closer to retirement age—or move through retirement—it's even more important that they remain invested in the changing circumstances of their individual financial world as well as the world around them. Estate planning certainly comes into play at this point; when clients are in retirement, we're coaching them to enjoy the time they have left with the fruits of their labor, and helping them shape the legacy that they wish to leave behind long after they're gone. But in the short-term, we want our clients to be able to know that we're the stewards of plans that will continue to make sense in changing times, particularly because their earning years are behind them. The risks are certainly higher when you have to live on a fixed income, and we take that seriously. Keeping our clients visiting us on a quarterly basis, at minimum, helps us in our efforts to stay on top of market changes, reassess risk, and keep unwanted surprises at bay.

## Are We the Only Ones? No, But...

I don't want to make it seem like my firm invented the quarterly meeting, because we didn't. But I will say this: while other advisors meet with clients on a quarterly basis, we offer a different ingredient, if you will. The frequency of meeting is an important gauge of how seriously your financial advisor might take you, but the different ingredient is that our plans (and thus, our meetings) are *comprehensive.*

In our meetings, we cover everything from financial planning, asset allocation, retirement income, social security, estate planning, and long-term care. We're not insurance salespeople, but we can't over-emphasize how important having appropriate long-term care planning is. One of the most insidious threats to your wealth is paying for nursing home or residential care; I know this from personal experience. My mother-in-law had been in a nursing home since 2010, paying $4,600 a month. That's close to $300,000 just on care costs alone at this point, not accounting for price increases. Thankfully, she properly planned for long-term care contingencies. If she hadn't, I don't know how we'd be able to maintain her level of care or her ability to leave an inheritance would have been diminished. Granny has since deceased and fortunately was able to leave her assets to her three daughters instead of using it to pay for her care. Proper planning just may make a big difference in you beneficiaries lives!

Keeping our meetings and the resulting financial plans comprehensive means that there's less opportunity for important information to slip through the cracks. An individual investor can't possibly know every piece of pertinent information that comprises a comprehensive financial plan—that's why they're paying guys like us, after all. We've found over the years that clients will unintentionally withhold information that they deem to be unimportant; they're not trying to do it to frustrate us or to shortchange themselves, but it's just the nature of the beast. Having regular check-ins resulting in a comprehensive plan can help counteract that tendency.

## How Our Quarterly Meetings Work

Some clients may appreciate having a 400-page pile of papers to hold open the door while they move heavy objects, but I have yet to meet someone who really takes the time to read and appreciate each page of such a plan. It's simply not possible for the average investor, nor is it a good use of that investor's time—by the time he gets through to the end, the plan will need to be revised! And it's a lot harder to revise a 400-page document than what we feel is a living, breathing 4-page plan—which is partially why those documents never get touched once the trees are dead and the pile is transformed into a doorstopper.

In our quarterly meetings, we present the client with their four-page plan—a simple, readable spreadsheet with a comprehensive overview of everything the client has under management. We then update those numbers where appropriate, and make recommendations where appropriate. Asset allocation and diversification are often part of this discussion; as trends shift and markets change, or as life circumstances dictate that we might need to free up funds or move more into a rainy-day reserve, we can easily make updates.

As we update these numbers, the client can see—in real time, in real dollar figures—how changes might impact their bottom line. Dealing with conservative assumptions, we can hypothetically show a client how much he may be able to expect to gain in a given year. Of course, markets will do what the markets will do, and there are no guarantees. But when we have our reporting structured in this way, we're able to answer "likely, yes" or "likely, no" to very important questions, like: "Will I have any money left in 2040?" A 400-page doorstop isn't going to give you that kind of clarity. And it's certainly not going to let you, the client, manipulate the numbers to glean information. That's why our firm also supplies an electronic version so that clients can go in and pose certain hypotheticals and see how these changes may affect them in the future. Suddenly, there's a lot less guesswork involved in buying a new car or planning to take that vacation they've been dreaming about.

We've found that it's easiest to achieve your goals if you can visualize them, and it's easiest to understand information if you can really *see* it. We've built a sample of what a plan might look like for two fictional clients, John and Amy Smith. If it looks simple and easy to understand, that's because it is. And if it still feels like you can't tell up from down, that's okay; we're going to keep breaking it down further as we go along together—in this book and, if you'd like, in our meetings.

## Asset Allocation

Below, you'll see an example[1] of what a very simple asset allocation spreadsheet might look like for our hypothetical couple. Notice

---

1 John and Amy are fictional characters and are not actual clients of Advanced Wealth Strategies. This case study does not reflect all factors that may influence the production of a financial plan for any specific client. Results do not reflect actual implementation of any financial plan and all the possible associated costs to do so. Material economic and market factors that may affect the design of a financial plan are also not reflected.

The information contained herein is for informational purposes only and should not be construed as investment advice or a recommendation to sell or buy any security or other investment, or undertake any investment strategy. It does not constitute a general or personal recommendation or take into account the particular investment objectives, financial situations, or needs of individual clients. Historical returns are not predictive of future results. Any investment involves significant risk, including a complete loss of capital and conflicts of interest.

that while the spreadsheet contains a bevy of information, it isn't overwhelming. We like to present this overview-type picture in our financial plans so that our clients can have a quick, realistic picture of what their assets look like. We've also included our recommendations for changes, which is what our clients see when they meet with us to update these living, breathing plans. The side-by-side comparison makes it easy to understand where the changes will occur, should they agree with us on the best course of action.

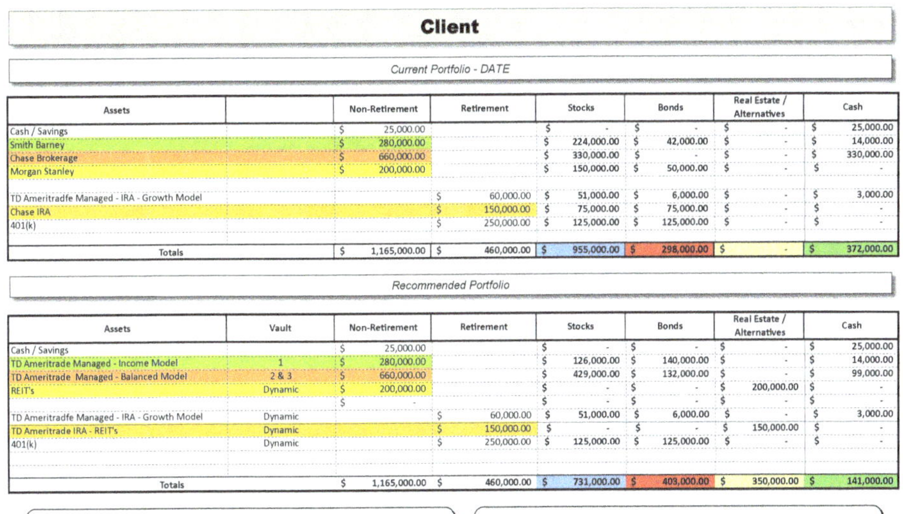

### Client

#### Current Portfolio - DATE

| Assets | | Non-Retirement | Retirement | Stocks | Bonds | Real Estate / Alternatives | Cash |
|---|---|---|---|---|---|---|---|
| Cash / Savings | | $ 25,000.00 | | $ - | $ - | $ - | $ 25,000.00 |
| Smith Barney | | $ 280,000.00 | | $ 224,000.00 | $ 42,000.00 | $ - | $ 14,000.00 |
| Chase Brokerage | | $ 660,000.00 | | $ 330,000.00 | $ - | $ - | $ 330,000.00 |
| Morgan Stanley | | $ 200,000.00 | | $ 150,000.00 | $ 50,000.00 | $ - | $ - |
| | | | | | | | |
| TD Ameritradfe Managed - IRA - Growth Model | | | $ 60,000.00 | $ 51,000.00 | $ 6,000.00 | $ - | $ 3,000.00 |
| Chase IRA | | | $ 150,000.00 | $ 75,000.00 | $ 75,000.00 | $ - | $ - |
| 401(k) | | | $ 250,000.00 | $ 125,000.00 | $ 125,000.00 | $ - | $ - |
| **Totals** | | $ 1,165,000.00 | $ 460,000.00 | $ 955,000.00 | $ 298,000.00 | $ - | $ 372,000.00 |

#### Recommended Portfolio

| Assets | Vault | Non-Retirement | Retirement | Stocks | Bonds | Real Estate / Alternatives | Cash |
|---|---|---|---|---|---|---|---|
| Cash / Savings | | $ 25,000.00 | | $ - | $ - | $ - | $ 25,000.00 |
| TD Ameritrade Managed - Income Model | 1 | $ 280,000.00 | | $ 126,000.00 | $ 140,000.00 | $ - | $ 14,000.00 |
| TD Ameritrade Managed - Balanced Model | 2 & 3 | $ 660,000.00 | | $ 429,000.00 | $ 132,000.00 | $ - | $ 99,000.00 |
| REIT's | Dynamic | $ 200,000.00 | | $ - | $ - | $ 200,000.00 | $ - |
| | | $ - | | $ - | $ - | $ - | $ - |
| TD Ameritradfe Managed - IRA - Growth Model | Dynamic | | $ 60,000.00 | $ 51,000.00 | $ 6,000.00 | $ - | $ 3,000.00 |
| TD Ameritrade IRA - REIT's | Dynamic | | $ 150,000.00 | $ - | $ - | $ 150,000.00 | $ - |
| 401(k) | Dynamic | | $ 250,000.00 | $ 125,000.00 | $ 125,000.00 | $ - | $ - |
| **Totals** | | $ 1,165,000.00 | $ 460,000.00 | $ 731,000.00 | $ 403,000.00 | $ 350,000.00 | $ 141,000.00 |

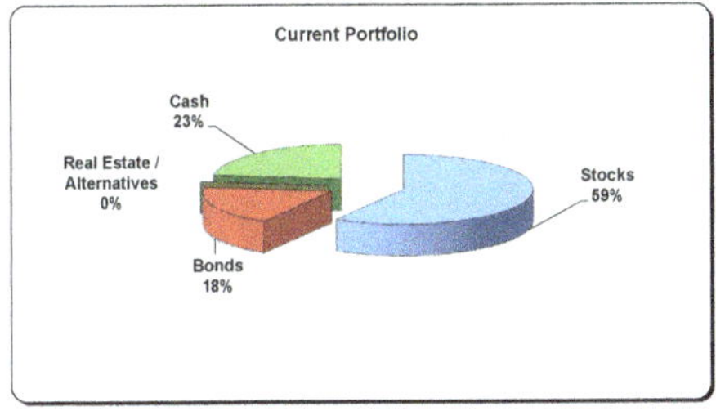


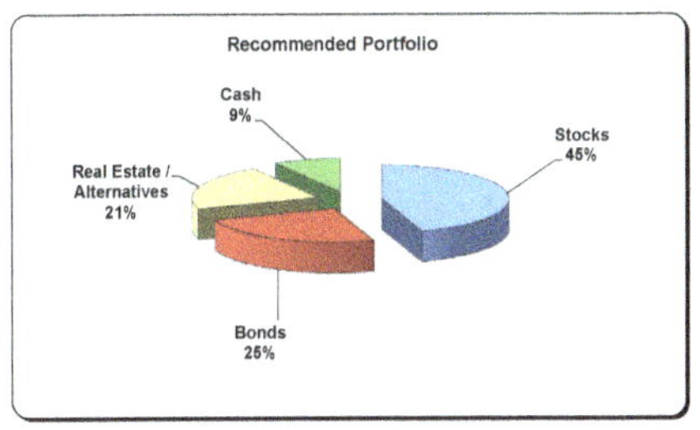

## Basic Analysis of Retirement

Below, we've shown John and Amy what their retirement might look like, adjusted for inflation, based on the assets shown above. You can see we've clearly broken out their expenses as well as their income, and gave a hypothetical rate of return on their investments: 5%. While we can never guarantee performance, we think that this rate of return is reasonable. If you are working with a financial advisor who promises you 10, 12, 15% or more on your investment returns during retirement, you need to run, not walk, out the door!

*[Continue to the next page to see example]*

## Client: John & Amy
### Hypothetical Retirement Analysis

**Assumptions**

| | |
|---|---|
| Current Age - John | 55 |
| Current Age - Amy | 53 |
| Retirement Age - John | 65 |
| Retirement Age - Amy | 65 |
| Annual Retirement Expenses | $ 125,000.00 Present Value |
| Inflation Rate | 3.00% |
| Social Security Inflation Rate | 2.00% |
| *Hypothetical Investment Rate of Return* | 5.00% |
| John Pension Income | $ 36,000.00 Present Value |
| *Annual Pre-Retirement Savings | $ 25,000.00 Present Value |
| Amy Pension Income | $ 20,000.00 Present Value |

**Assets**

| | |
|---|---|
| #REF! | $ 1,165,000.00 |
| #REF! | $ 460,000.00 |
| Investment Total | $ 1,625,000.00 |

Retirement Analysis

| Year | Annual Retirement Expenses | Lump Sum Expenses | Total Expenses | *Annual Pre-Retirement Savings | Social Security Income - John | Social Security Income - Amy | John Pension Income | Amy Pension Income | Investment Income | Total Income | **Investment Balance |
|---|---|---|---|---|---|---|---|---|---|---|---|
| 1 | $ - | | $ - | $ 25,000.00 | $ - | $ - | $ - | $ - | $ - | $ - | $1,731,250.00 |
| 2 | $ - | | $ - | $ 25,750.00 | $ - | $ - | $ - | $ - | $ - | $ - | $1,843,562.50 |
| 3 | $ - | | $ - | $ 26,522.50 | $ - | $ - | $ - | $ - | $ - | $ - | $1,962,263.13 |
| 4 | $ - | | $ - | $ 27,318.18 | $ - | $ - | $ - | $ - | $ - | $ - | $2,087,694.46 |
| 5 | $ - | | $ - | $ 28,137.72 | $ - | $ - | $ - | $ - | $ - | $ - | $2,220,216.90 |
| 6 | $ - | | $ - | $ 28,981.85 | $ - | $ - | $ - | $ - | $ - | $ - | $2,360,209.60 |
| 7 | $ - | | $ - | $ 29,851.31 | $ - | $ - | $ - | $ - | $ - | $ - | $2,508,071.38 |
| 8 | $ - | | $ - | $ 30,746.85 | $ - | $ - | $ - | $ - | $ - | $ - | $2,664,221.80 |
| 9 | $ - | | $ - | $ 31,669.25 | $ - | $ - | $ - | $ - | $ - | $ - | $2,829,102.14 |
| 10 | $ - | | $ - | $ 32,619.33 | $ - | $ - | $ - | $ - | $ - | $ - | $3,003,176.58 |
| 11 | $ 167,989.55 | | $ 167,989.55 | $ - | $ 20,000.00 | $ - | $ 36,000.00 | $ - | 111,989.55 | $ 167,989.55 | $3,041,345.86 |
| 12 | $ 173,029.23 | | $ 173,029.23 | $ - | $ 20,400.00 | $ - | $ 36,000.00 | $ - | 116,629.23 | $ 173,029.23 | $3,076,783.92 |
| 13 | $ 178,220.11 | | $ 178,220.11 | $ - | $ 20,808.00 | $ 18,000.00 | $ 36,000.00 | $ 20,000.00 | 83,412.11 | $ 178,220.11 | $3,147,211.00 |
| 14 | $ 183,566.71 | | $ 183,566.71 | $ - | $ 21,224.16 | $ 18,360.00 | $ 36,000.00 | $ 20,000.00 | 87,982.55 | $ 183,566.71 | $3,216,589.00 |
| 15 | $ 189,073.72 | | $ 189,073.72 | $ - | $ 21,648.64 | $ 18,727.20 | $ 36,000.00 | $ 20,000.00 | 92,697.87 | $ 189,073.72 | $3,284,720.58 |
| 16 | $ 194,745.93 | | $ 194,745.93 | $ - | $ 22,081.62 | $ 19,101.74 | $ 36,000.00 | $ 20,000.00 | 97,562.57 | $ 194,745.93 | $3,351,394.04 |
| 17 | $ 200,588.30 | | $ 200,588.30 | $ - | $ 22,523.25 | $ 19,483.78 | $ 36,000.00 | $ 20,000.00 | 102,581.28 | $ 200,588.30 | $3,416,382.46 |
| 18 | $ 206,605.95 | | $ 206,605.95 | $ - | $ 22,973.71 | $ 19,873.45 | $ 36,000.00 | $ 20,000.00 | 107,758.79 | $ 206,605.95 | $3,479,442.80 |
| 19 | $ 212,804.13 | | $ 212,804.13 | $ - | $ 23,433.19 | $ 20,270.92 | $ 36,000.00 | $ 20,000.00 | 113,100.02 | $ 212,804.13 | $3,540,314.92 |
| 20 | $ 219,188.26 | | $ 219,188.26 | $ - | $ 23,901.85 | $ 20,676.34 | $ 36,000.00 | $ 20,000.00 | 118,610.06 | $ 219,188.26 | $3,598,720.60 |
| 21 | $ 225,763.90 | | $ 225,763.90 | $ - | $ 24,379.89 | $ 21,089.87 | $ 36,000.00 | $ 20,000.00 | 124,294.15 | $ 225,763.90 | $3,654,362.48 |
| 22 | $ 232,536.82 | | $ 232,536.82 | $ - | $ 24,867.49 | $ 21,511.67 | $ 36,000.00 | $ 20,000.00 | 130,157.67 | $ 232,536.82 | $3,706,922.94 |
| 23 | $ 239,512.93 | | $ 239,512.93 | $ - | $ 25,364.84 | $ 21,941.90 | $ 36,000.00 | $ 20,000.00 | 136,206.19 | $ 239,512.93 | $3,756,062.90 |
| 24 | $ 246,698.31 | | $ 246,698.31 | $ - | $ 25,872.13 | $ 22,380.74 | $ 36,000.00 | $ 20,000.00 | 142,445.44 | $ 246,698.31 | $3,801,420.60 |
| 25 | $ 254,099.26 | | $ 254,099.26 | $ - | $ 26,389.58 | $ 22,828.35 | $ 36,000.00 | $ 20,000.00 | 148,881.34 | $ 254,099.26 | $3,842,610.29 |
| 26 | $ 261,722.24 | | $ 261,722.24 | $ - | $ 26,917.37 | $ 23,284.92 | $ 36,000.00 | $ 20,000.00 | 155,519.96 | $ 261,722.24 | $3,879,220.85 |
| 27 | $ 269,573.91 | | $ 269,573.91 | $ - | $ 27,455.71 | $ 23,750.62 | $ 36,000.00 | $ 20,000.00 | 162,367.58 | $ 269,573.91 | $3,910,814.32 |
| 28 | $ 277,661.13 | | $ 277,661.13 | $ - | $ 28,004.83 | $ 24,225.63 | $ 36,000.00 | $ 20,000.00 | 169,430.67 | $ 277,661.13 | $3,936,924.36 |
| 29 | $ 285,990.96 | | $ 285,990.96 | $ - | $ 28,564.92 | $ 24,710.14 | $ 36,000.00 | $ 20,000.00 | 176,715.89 | $ 285,990.96 | $3,957,054.69 |
| 30 | $ 294,570.69 | | $ 294,570.69 | $ - | $ 29,136.22 | $ 25,204.35 | $ 36,000.00 | $ 20,000.00 | 184,230.12 | $ 294,570.69 | $3,970,677.31 |
| 31 | $ 303,407.81 | | $ 303,407.81 | $ - | $ 29,718.95 | $ 25,708.43 | $ 36,000.00 | $ 20,000.00 | 191,980.43 | $ 303,407.81 | $3,977,230.74 |
| 32 | $ 312,510.04 | | $ 312,510.04 | $ - | $ 30,313.33 | $ 26,222.60 | $ 36,000.00 | $ 20,000.00 | 199,974.12 | $ 312,510.04 | $3,976,118.17 |
| 33 | $ 321,885.34 | | $ 321,885.34 | $ - | $ 30,919.59 | $ 26,747.05 | $ 36,000.00 | $ 20,000.00 | 208,218.70 | $ 321,885.34 | $3,966,705.38 |
| 34 | $ 331,541.90 | | $ 331,541.90 | $ - | $ 31,537.99 | $ 27,281.99 | $ 36,000.00 | $ 20,000.00 | 216,721.93 | $ 331,541.90 | $3,948,318.72 |
| 35 | $ 341,488.16 | | $ 341,488.16 | $ - | $ 32,168.74 | $ 27,827.63 | $ 36,000.00 | $ 20,000.00 | 225,491.78 | $ 341,488.16 | $3,920,242.87 |
| 36 | $ 351,732.81 | | $ 351,732.81 | $ - | $ 32,812.12 | $ 28,384.19 | $ 36,000.00 | $ 20,000.00 | 234,536.50 | $ 351,732.81 | $3,881,718.52 |
| 37 | $ 362,284.79 | | $ 362,284.79 | $ - | $ 33,468.36 | $ 28,951.87 | $ 36,000.00 | $ 20,000.00 | 243,864.56 | $ 362,284.79 | $3,831,939.88 |
| 38 | $ 373,153.33 | | $ 373,153.33 | $ - | $ 34,137.73 | $ 29,530.91 | $ 36,000.00 | $ 20,000.00 | 253,484.70 | $ 373,153.33 | $3,770,052.18 |
| 39 | $ 384,347.93 | | $ 384,347.93 | $ - | $ 34,820.48 | $ 30,121.53 | $ 36,000.00 | $ 20,000.00 | 263,405.92 | $ 384,347.93 | $3,695,148.86 |
| 40 | $ 395,878.37 | | $ 395,878.37 | $ - | $ 35,516.89 | $ 30,723.96 | $ 36,000.00 | $ 20,000.00 | 273,637.52 | $ 395,878.37 | $3,606,268.79 |
| 41 | $ 407,754.72 | | $ 407,754.72 | $ - | $ 36,227.23 | $ 31,338.44 | $ 36,000.00 | $ 20,000.00 | 284,189.06 | $ 407,754.72 | $3,502,393.17 |
| 42 | $ 419,987.37 | | $ 419,987.37 | $ - | $ 36,951.78 | $ 31,965.20 | $ 36,000.00 | $ 20,000.00 | 295,070.38 | $ 419,987.37 | $3,382,442.44 |
| 43 | $ 432,586.99 | | $ 432,586.99 | $ - | $ 37,690.81 | $ 32,604.51 | $ 36,000.00 | $ 20,000.00 | 306,291.67 | $ 432,586.99 | $3,245,272.90 |
| 44 | $ 445,564.60 | | $ 445,564.60 | $ - | $ 38,444.63 | $ 33,256.60 | $ 36,000.00 | $ 20,000.00 | 317,863.37 | $ 445,564.60 | $3,089,673.17 |
| 45 | $ 458,931.53 | | $ 458,931.53 | $ - | $ 39,213.52 | $ 33,921.73 | $ 36,000.00 | $ 20,000.00 | 329,796.28 | $ 458,931.53 | $2,914,360.55 |
| 46 | $ 472,699.48 | | $ 472,699.48 | $ - | $ 39,997.79 | $ 34,600.17 | $ 36,000.00 | $ 20,000.00 | 342,101.52 | $ 472,699.48 | $2,717,977.05 |

This analysis will be based on the information and assumptions that you provided. You should not use it to obtain credit or for any purposes other than financial planning.

Any tax aspects presented are for illustration only, and are based on current federal tax law and assumed tax rates.

Depicted rates of return are hypothetical and are not representative of the actual rate of return that you will experience with any particular insurance or financial product.
Actual results will vary depending on the insurance or financial product you purchase, the amount of premiums or payments you make, the benefits, charges, expenses, guaranteed (if any) and non-guaranteed elements of the policy or product, and general market conditions.
Asset allocation does not ensure a profit or protect against losses in a declining market. Investments offering the potential for higher rates of return also involve a higher degree of risk. Actual results will vary.

IMPORTANT: The projections or other information generated by this analysis regarding the likelihood of various investment outcomes are hypothetical in nature, do not reflect actual investment results and are not guarantees of future results.

Advanced Wealth Strategies Group is a branch office of DFPG Investments Inc. Investment Advisory Services offered through Integrated Advisors Network LLC, a registered investment advisor. Securities offered through DFPG Investments Inc,
member FINRA/SIPC. DFPG Investments Inc and Integrated Advisors Network LLC are not affiliated. www.finra.org www.sipc.org

Social Security and pension income are subject to the claims-paying ability of the U.S. Government and/or pension guarantor, respectively.

* Annual Pre-Retirement Savings - This is your current annual investment savings, whether it is in your company retirement plan, bank, etc. Each year this value increases with the assumed inflation rate.

**Investment Balance - The investment balance is calculated by taking your current investment balance times the "Hypothetical Investment Rate of Return", less the Investment Income", plus the "Annual Pre-Retirement Savings".

## Client. John & Amy
### Hypothetical Retirement Analysis

| Assumptions | | |
|---|---|---|
| Current Age - John | 55 | |
| Current Age - Amy | 53 | |
| Retirement Age - John | 65 | |
| Retirement Age - Amy | 65 | |
| Annual Retirement Expenses | $ 125,000.00 | Present Value |
| Inflation Rate | 3.00% | |
| Social Security Inflation Rate | 2.00% | |
| *Hypothetical Investment Rate of Return* | -1.50% | |
| John Pension Income | $ 36,000.00 | Present Value |
| *Annual Pre-Retirement Savings | $ 25,000.00 | Present Value |
| Amy Pension Income | $ 20,000.00 | Present Value |

**Rate of return Assumtion is -1.5% which represents
a 0% rate of return and 1.5% management fee**

| Assets | | |
|---|---|---|
| #REF! | $ | 1,165,000.00 |
| #REF! | $ | 460,000.00 |
| 0 | $ | - |
| 0 | $ | - |
| 0 | $ | - |
| 0 | $ | - |
| 0 | $ | - |
| | $ | - |
| | $ | - |
| | $ | - |
| | $ | - |
| | $ | - |
| | $ | - |
| Investment Total | $ | 1,625,000.00 |

Retirement Analysis

| Year | Annual Retirement Expenses | Lump Sum Expenses | Total Expenses | *Annual Pre-Retirement Savings | Social Security Income - John | Social Security Income - Amy | John Pension Income | Amy Pension Income | Investment Income | Total Income | **Investment Balance |
|---|---|---|---|---|---|---|---|---|---|---|---|
| 1 | $ - | $ - | $ - | $ 25,000.00 | $ - | $ - | $ - | $ - | $ - | $ - | $1,625,625.00 |
| 2 | $ - | $ - | $ - | $ 25,750.00 | $ - | $ - | $ - | $ - | $ - | $ - | $1,626,990.63 |
| 3 | $ - | $ - | $ - | $ 26,522.50 | $ - | $ - | $ - | $ - | $ - | $ - | $1,629,108.27 |
| 4 | $ - | $ - | $ - | $ 27,318.18 | $ - | $ - | $ - | $ - | $ - | $ - | $1,631,989.82 |
| 5 | $ - | $ - | $ - | $ 28,137.72 | $ - | $ - | $ - | $ - | $ - | $ - | $1,635,647.69 |
| 6 | $ - | $ - | $ - | $ 28,981.85 | $ - | $ - | $ - | $ - | $ - | $ - | $1,640,094.83 |
| 7 | $ - | $ - | $ - | $ 29,851.31 | $ - | $ - | $ - | $ - | $ - | $ - | $1,645,344.71 |
| 8 | $ - | $ - | $ - | $ 30,746.85 | $ - | $ - | $ - | $ - | $ - | $ - | $1,651,411.39 |
| 9 | $ - | $ - | $ - | $ 31,669.25 | $ - | $ - | $ - | $ - | $ - | $ - | $1,658,309.47 |
| 10 | $ - | $ - | $ - | $ 32,619.33 | $ - | $ - | $ - | $ - | $ - | $ - | $1,666,054.16 |
| 11 | $ 167,989.55 | $ - | $ 167,989.55 | $ - | $ 20,000.00 | $ - | $ 36,000.00 | $ - | $ 111,989.55 | $ 167,989.55 | $1,529,073.80 |
| 12 | $ 173,029.23 | $ - | $ 173,029.23 | $ - | $ 20,400.00 | $ - | $ 36,000.00 | $ - | $ 116,629.23 | $ 173,029.23 | $1,389,508.46 |
| 13 | $ 178,220.11 | $ - | $ 178,220.11 | $ - | $ 20,808.00 | $ 18,000.00 | $ 36,000.00 | $ 20,000.00 | $ 83,412.11 | $ 178,220.11 | $1,285,253.72 |
| 14 | $ 183,566.71 | $ - | $ 183,566.71 | $ - | $ 21,224.16 | $ 18,360.00 | $ 36,000.00 | $ 20,000.00 | $ 87,982.55 | $ 183,566.71 | $1,177,992.36 |
| 15 | $ 189,073.72 | $ - | $ 189,073.72 | $ - | $ 21,648.64 | $ 18,727.20 | $ 36,000.00 | $ 20,000.00 | $ 92,697.87 | $ 189,073.72 | $1,067,624.60 |
| 16 | $ 194,745.93 | $ - | $ 194,745.93 | $ - | $ 22,081.62 | $ 19,101.74 | $ 36,000.00 | $ 20,000.00 | $ 97,562.57 | $ 194,745.93 | $954,047.66 |
| 17 | $ 200,588.30 | $ - | $ 200,588.30 | $ - | $ 22,523.25 | $ 19,483.78 | $ 36,000.00 | $ 20,000.00 | $ 102,581.28 | $ 200,588.30 | $837,155.67 |
| 18 | $ 206,605.95 | $ - | $ 206,605.95 | $ - | $ 22,973.71 | $ 19,873.45 | $ 36,000.00 | $ 20,000.00 | $ 107,758.79 | $ 206,605.95 | $716,839.55 |
| 19 | $ 212,804.13 | $ - | $ 212,804.13 | $ - | $ 23,433.19 | $ 20,270.92 | $ 36,000.00 | $ 20,000.00 | $ 113,100.02 | $ 212,804.13 | $592,986.94 |
| 20 | $ 219,188.26 | $ - | $ 219,188.26 | $ - | $ 23,901.85 | $ 20,676.34 | $ 36,000.00 | $ 20,000.00 | $ 118,610.06 | $ 219,188.26 | $465,482.07 |
| 21 | $ 225,763.90 | $ - | $ 225,763.90 | $ - | $ 24,379.89 | $ 21,089.87 | $ 36,000.00 | $ 20,000.00 | $ 124,294.15 | $ 225,763.90 | $334,205.69 |
| 22 | $ 232,536.82 | $ - | $ 232,536.82 | $ - | $ 24,867.49 | $ 21,511.67 | $ 36,000.00 | $ 20,000.00 | $ 130,157.67 | $ 232,536.82 | $199,034.94 |
| 23 | $ 239,512.93 | $ - | $ 239,512.93 | $ - | $ 25,364.84 | $ 21,941.90 | $ 36,000.00 | $ 20,000.00 | $ 136,206.19 | $ 239,512.93 | $59,843.22 |
| 24 | $ 246,698.31 | $ - | $ 246,698.31 | $ - | $ 25,872.13 | $ 22,380.74 | $ 36,000.00 | $ 20,000.00 | $ 142,445.44 | $ 246,698.31 | ($83,499.87) |
| 25 | $ 254,099.26 | $ - | $ 254,099.26 | $ - | $ 26,389.58 | $ 22,828.35 | $ 36,000.00 | $ 20,000.00 | $ 148,881.34 | $ 254,099.26 | ($231,128.71) |
| 26 | $ 261,722.24 | $ - | $ 261,722.24 | $ - | $ 26,917.37 | $ 23,284.92 | $ 36,000.00 | $ 20,000.00 | $ 155,519.96 | $ 261,722.24 | ($383,181.73) |
| 27 | $ 269,573.91 | $ - | $ 269,573.91 | $ - | $ 27,455.71 | $ 23,750.62 | $ 36,000.00 | $ 20,000.00 | $ 162,367.58 | $ 269,573.91 | ($539,801.58) |
| 28 | $ 277,661.13 | $ - | $ 277,661.13 | $ - | $ 28,004.83 | $ 24,225.63 | $ 36,000.00 | $ 20,000.00 | $ 169,430.67 | $ 277,661.13 | ($701,135.23) |
| 29 | $ 285,990.96 | $ - | $ 285,990.96 | $ - | $ 28,564.92 | $ 24,710.14 | $ 36,000.00 | $ 20,000.00 | $ 176,715.89 | $ 285,990.96 | ($867,334.09) |
| 30 | $ 294,570.69 | $ - | $ 294,570.69 | $ - | $ 29,136.22 | $ 25,204.35 | $ 36,000.00 | $ 20,000.00 | $ 184,230.12 | $ 294,570.69 | ($1,038,554.20) |
| 31 | $ 303,407.81 | $ - | $ 303,407.81 | $ - | $ 29,718.95 | $ 25,708.43 | $ 36,000.00 | $ 20,000.00 | $ 191,980.43 | $ 303,407.81 | ($1,214,956.31) |
| 32 | $ 312,510.04 | $ - | $ 312,510.04 | $ - | $ 30,313.33 | $ 26,222.60 | $ 36,000.00 | $ 20,000.00 | $ 199,974.12 | $ 312,510.04 | ($1,396,706.08) |
| 33 | $ 321,885.34 | $ - | $ 321,885.34 | $ - | $ 30,919.59 | $ 26,747.05 | $ 36,000.00 | $ 20,000.00 | $ 208,218.70 | $ 321,885.34 | ($1,583,974.19) |
| 34 | $ 331,541.90 | $ - | $ 331,541.90 | $ - | $ 31,537.99 | $ 27,281.99 | $ 36,000.00 | $ 20,000.00 | $ 216,721.93 | $ 331,541.90 | ($1,776,936.50) |
| 35 | $ 341,488.16 | $ - | $ 341,488.16 | $ - | $ 32,168.74 | $ 27,827.63 | $ 36,000.00 | $ 20,000.00 | $ 225,491.78 | $ 341,488.16 | ($1,975,774.24) |
| 36 | $ 351,732.81 | $ - | $ 351,732.81 | $ - | $ 32,812.12 | $ 28,384.19 | $ 36,000.00 | $ 20,000.00 | $ 234,536.50 | $ 351,732.81 | ($2,180,674.13) |
| 37 | $ 362,284.79 | $ - | $ 362,284.79 | $ - | $ 33,468.36 | $ 28,951.87 | $ 36,000.00 | $ 20,000.00 | $ 243,864.56 | $ 362,284.79 | ($2,391,828.57) |
| 38 | $ 373,153.33 | $ - | $ 373,153.33 | $ - | $ 34,137.73 | $ 29,530.91 | $ 36,000.00 | $ 20,000.00 | $ 253,484.70 | $ 373,153.33 | ($2,609,435.84) |
| 39 | $ 384,347.93 | $ - | $ 384,347.93 | $ - | $ 34,820.48 | $ 30,121.53 | $ 36,000.00 | $ 20,000.00 | $ 263,405.92 | $ 384,347.93 | ($2,833,760.23) |
| 40 | $ 395,878.37 | $ - | $ 395,878.37 | $ - | $ 35,516.89 | $ 30,723.96 | $ 36,000.00 | $ 20,000.00 | $ 273,637.52 | $ 395,878.37 | ($3,064,832.25) |
| 41 | $ 407,754.72 | $ - | $ 407,754.72 | $ - | $ 36,227.23 | $ 31,338.44 | $ 36,000.00 | $ 20,000.00 | $ 284,189.06 | $ 407,754.72 | ($3,303,048.82) |
| 42 | $ 419,987.37 | $ - | $ 419,987.37 | $ - | $ 36,951.78 | $ 31,965.20 | $ 36,000.00 | $ 20,000.00 | $ 295,070.38 | $ 419,987.37 | ($3,548,573.47) |
| 43 | $ 432,586.99 | $ - | $ 432,586.99 | $ - | $ 37,690.81 | $ 32,604.51 | $ 36,000.00 | $ 20,000.00 | $ 306,291.67 | $ 432,586.99 | ($3,801,636.54) |
| 44 | $ 445,564.60 | $ - | $ 445,564.60 | $ - | $ 38,444.63 | $ 33,256.60 | $ 36,000.00 | $ 20,000.00 | $ 317,863.37 | $ 445,564.60 | ($4,062,475.36) |
| 45 | $ 458,931.53 | $ - | $ 458,931.53 | $ - | $ 39,213.52 | $ 33,921.73 | $ 36,000.00 | $ 20,000.00 | $ 329,796.28 | $ 458,931.53 | ($4,331,334.51) |
| 46 | $ 472,699.48 | $ - | $ 472,699.48 | $ - | $ 39,997.79 | $ 34,600.17 | $ 36,000.00 | $ 20,000.00 | $ 342,101.52 | $ 472,699.48 | ($4,608,466.02) |

This analysis will be based on the information and assumptions that you provided. You should not use it to obtain credit or for any purposes other than financial planning.
Any tax aspects presented are for illustration only, and are based on current federal tax law and assumed tax rates.

Depicted rates of return are hypothetical and are not representative of the actual rate of return that you will experience with any particular insurance or financial product.
Actual results will vary depending on the insurance or financial product you purchase, the amount of premiums or payments you make, the benefits, charges, expenses, guaranteed (if any) and non-guaranteed elements of the policy or product, and general market conditions.
Asset allocation does not ensure a profit or protect against losses in a declining market. Investments offering the potential for higher rates of return also involve a higher degree of risk. Actual results will vary.

IMPORTANT: The projections or other information generated by this analysis regarding the likelihood of various investment outcomes are hypothetical in nature, do not reflect actual investment results and are not guarantees of future results.

Advanced Wealth Strategies Group is a branch office of DFPG Investments Inc. Investment Advisory Services offered through Integrated Advisors Network LLC, a registered investment advisor. Securities offered through DFPG Investments Inc,
member FINRA/SIPC. DFPG Investments Inc and Integrated Advisors Network LLC are not affiliated. www.finra.org www.sipc.org

Social Security and pension income are subject to the claims-paying ability of the U.S. Government and/or pension guarantor, respectively.

* Annual Pre-Retirement Savings - This is your current annual investment savings, whether it is in your company retirement plan, bank, etc. Each year this value increases with the assumed inflation rate.

**Investment Balance - The investment balance is calculated by taking your current Investment balance times the "Hypothetical Investment Rate of Return", less the Investment Income", plus the "Annual Pre-Retirement Savings".

# CHAPTER FIVE

# Phases and Vaults

**N**O MATTER WHAT YOUR FINANCIAL SITUATION, ONE OF the biggest issues that we face when we start to think about retirement is the notion of how we want to spend that time. Do we plan to take vacations and travel the world? Do we want to take up a new hobby, like golf or fishing, and plan our schedules and even location around that hobby? Although these questions aren't strictly financial, the philosophical and logistical concerns they address do have financial implications. To address both sides of these issues of retirement, we help our clients plan their retirement in terms of *phases* and *vaults*.

## The Three Phases of Retirement: Go Go Time, Go Slow Time, and No Go Time

Although retirement looks different for everyone (and that's why we shy away from one-size-fits-all plans!), over the years, our experience with clients has led us to differentiate three typical phases of retirement. Each of these phases of retirement has different financial needs, and are largely structured on the level of activity that typically takes place during each one.

The first phase—right after retirement—is the ever-exciting *go go time*. Ideally, it should be as fun as it sounds! This is when you're still fairly young (and young at heart), and when you've got the physical capability to tackle some of the more challenging goals on your bucket list. With the nest empty and the hours suddenly your own to enjoy, you've got a lot to look forward to during this time.

We tell our clients that this phase typically lasts for the first ten years of their retirement. It's not uncommon for us to have big dreamers who have trouble pulling the trigger, thinking that there's going to be a better or more convenient time to take that trip to Europe or sail down to the Bahamas. And while we would never push someone beyond his or her comfort zone, we do encourage our clients to not put off these go-go time plans for too long. The reality is that time is taking its toll, and you or your spouse may face significant long- or short-term health issues in the near future. These issues will likely be problematic not just from a logistical standpoint, but from a financial standpoint as well. If and when they arise, your financial focus will be on addressing those problems, and we can't count on Medicare to foot all of those bills. So the time to get up and go is definitely during the go-go time.

In this initial period of retirement, we find that our clients will often try to get a handle on their spending needs, while also figuring out how they'll enjoy this phase. What looks good at the beginning of the journey might not necessarily look so good six or seven months in, for example. It's important to note that we start with projections, and still rely on our quarterly meetings to make adjustments along the way. There are no right or wrong answers for how to approach retirement planning, and we know that those answers can shift for everyone. Our projections are based on ideals, but we aim to make them conservative and reasonable ones, so that when the time comes to adjust, we have some room to do so.

The second phase of retirement is the *go slow time.* During this phase, clients may typically want to spend more time with family (spoiling your grandkids is much easier when you're retired and don't have to plan vacations around work), decrease the length and intensity of trips, and so on. In the best of all possible worlds, clients will still enjoy relative health during this period, but that can't be guaranteed by anyone, and as we age, even in the best of health, our mobility and stamina will decrease. *Go slow time* is a period when we encourage our clients to really focus on getting all their ducks in a row—making sure beneficiaries and powers of attorney are updated, adjusting their budgets and spending as necessary—so that they can continue to enjoy themselves without worrying about running out of money before they run out of time or leaving behind a maze of paperwork for their loved ones.

The final phase of our retirement may be least enjoyable to talk about, but that doesn't mean it needs to be entirely without its own comforts and benefits. *No go time* comes when we are either physically unable or are uninterested in the more taxing undertakings such as travel, an encore career or volunteer effort. It's our aim to make sure that clients have the financial resources that they need to make it through these years, whether that means covering basic living expenses or dealing with the consequences of expensive health issues. In either case, it's crucial to acknowledge the eventual existence of this period of time. We can't stick our heads in the sand and refuse to plan for the inevitable at any point, but this practice is particularly foolish when it comes to retirement planning, particularly in the no go time phase. In this phase, earning potential is gone, and we have to be able to rely on the fruits of our labor and planning from years past. Without it, both clients and those who care about them would be at an impossible impasse.

## The Adjustable Art of Projecting What You'll Need

Projections aren't an exact science, and even the best advisors (and clients) sometimes over-project what they're going to need in retirement. We try to keep our estimates conservative so that the wiggle room is available in the right direction—as we've talked about, earning potential is drastically reduced or eliminated in retirement, and a retired client won't be as resilient as a younger one when it comes to making up for shortcomings in the earnings/expenses department.

The old adage seems to say that when you retire, you'll need a fixed income that runs about half of what you're earning now. We find that a little too aggressive—some expenses will actually go *down* during retirement, such as the expenses associated with commuting (gas and car maintenance), wardrobe, professional development, and so on. But we don't want to start getting too high on the hog either. We find that in many cases, clients can live on 75 to 80 percent of what they earn each year, but the caveat is there, as always, that the number truly depends on what your retirement looks like—what you're doing, what your expenses are, if you're traveling or caring for an ailing spouse, etc.

Often, our clients don't yet know which expenses will go down and by how much, and so adjusting for these after a certain period makes sense. And having a surplus is a great problem to have! As advisors, we're fortunate that most of our clients are savers rather than spendthrifts. There's a reason they've been able to make it to the level where they can benefit from our advice, and it all starts with good saving habits. The younger generations, although we don't deal with too many folks under fifty, would do well to take heed of these saving habits of their elders, particularly as the systems in place in the Federal Government may not be able to take care of us twenty or thirty years down the line nearly as much as they do now. Contrary to what the masses might think, relying solely on a safety net is not enough!

The neat thing about our quarterly meetings is that it allows us built-in time to discuss and adjust. We'll typically have set up automatic distributions of the appropriate amount to a clients' checking account (partially to ensure a seamless deposit process when our clients are traveling!), so when we meet by the quarter, we'll see if we need to turn the faucet up or slow it down. We'll ask questions about the client's health, or any special needs that may have arisen, or whether or not they're planning to make a big purchase in the future (think automobiles, second homes, or that trip around the world they've been dreaming of).

## Striving for Safety:
## Segmenting Assets into Vaults

You've probably heard of segmentation strategies before, most commonly referred to as "buckets" of money. It's when an advisor takes a look at all of your assets in total and breaks them down into separate compartments, with the idea that each compartment is meant to be used during a specific time.

We like to call these compartments vaults, because of the obvious connotations of safety and security. While we obviously can't make any guarantees about safety, that's not what we're getting at. Rather, we like our clients to think of these asset groupings as places where they are storing money away for brighter days and rainy futures in equal measure.

We break these vaults down into four time segments:

- **1 to 3 years.** We think of this vault as being the money that you're really going to need to use right away. You'll also be spending this period of retirement adjusting your expectations and income as you see what your expenses and liabilities will be. Some of our clients never take any income, not in this stage or ever—they're fortunate to have great pensions, or more than ample social security benefits. But nowadays, unfortunately, it's common for pensions to be underfunded or unfunded, leaving each client to attend to his or her own individual retirement. Therefore, this vault and the three remaining vaults become even more crucial. In the one- to three-year vault, we'll put the funds in low-volatility asset classes: CDs, short-term bonds, and government securities, for example.[1] We're not looking for a big return with these vehicles, but rather a short-term place to park money that will be needed relatively quickly. We want a little bit of growth if we can get it, so that we can adjust for our fees and inflation, and avoid a negative drawdown for the client. But we're not talking major returns here.

- **3 to 7 years.** We think of this vault as the balance-building period. Hopefully we've been able to sleep at night knowing that the immediate expenses were parked in a lower-risk place, and that our clients have had those immediate needs satisfied.

- **8 to 15 years.** In this vault, we take a balanced approach that typically ends up being somewhere around 60 percent in different types of stocks and ETFs, while around 40 percent goes to income producing products like bonds.[2] We want clients to get some of both worlds in this vault.

- **15+ years.** We call this vault the Dynasty vault for a reason. We're trying to be as growth-oriented as we possibly can, which may increase risk, in an effort to replace the money that we've spent in the first fifteen years of retirement, not just for the client, but for their heirs, as well.

---

1 All investments involve a certain degree of risk.
2 All investments involve a certain degree of risk.

**Client, John and Amy**

*Annual Retirement Investment Income Report*

| Total Investment | | | $3,003,176.58 |
|---|---|---|---|

| | | Income Vault | | Vault 1[1] | Vault 2[2] | Vault 3[3] | Dynamic Vault[4] |
|---|---|---|---|---|---|---|---|
| | Allocation of Investment | 3.33% | | 9.76% | 10.28% | 18.52% | 58.12% |
| | Annual Net Rate of Return* | | | 1.50% | 3.50% | 5.50% | 6.50% |
| Retirement Year | Monthly Income Required | VA w/5% Guaranteed Income[5] | | Years 1-3 | Years 4-7 | Years 8-15 | Years 15 + |
| Retirement Date Beginning Balance | | $ 100,000.00 | | $293,080.72 | $308,586.77 | $556,067.51 | $1,745,441.58 |
| 1 | $ 9,332.46 | $ 416.67 | | $ (106,989.55) | $ 319,387.31 | $ 586,651.22 | $ 1,858,895.28 |
| 2 | $ 9,719.10 | $ 416.67 | | $ (111,629.23) | $ 330,565.86 | $ 618,917.04 | $ 1,979,723.47 |
| 3 | $ 6,951.01 | $ 416.67 | | $ (78,412.11) | $ 342,135.67 | $ 652,957.47 | $ 2,108,405.50 |
| 4 | $ 7,331.88 | $ 416.67 | | $ - | $ (82,982.55) | $ 688,870.14 | $ 2,245,451.86 |
| 5 | $ 7,724.82 | $ 416.67 | | $ - | $ (87,697.87) | $ 726,757.99 | $ 2,391,406.23 |
| 6 | $ 8,130.21 | $ 416.67 | | $ - | $ (92,562.57) | $ 766,729.68 | $ 2,546,847.63 |
| 7 | $ 8,548.44 | $ 416.67 | | $ - | $ (97,581.28) | $ 808,899.81 | $ 2,712,392.73 |
| 8 | $ 8,979.90 | $ 416.67 | | $ - | $ - | $ (102,758.79) | $ 2,888,698.26 |
| 9 | $ 9,425.00 | $ 416.67 | | $ - | $ - | $ (108,100.02) | $ 3,076,463.64 |
| 10 | $ 9,884.17 | $ 416.67 | | $ - | $ - | $ (113,610.06) | $ 3,276,433.78 |
| 11 | $ 10,357.85 | $ 416.67 | | $ - | $ - | $ (119,294.15) | $ 3,489,401.97 |
| 12 | $ 10,846.47 | $ 416.67 | | $ - | $ - | $ (125,157.67) | $ 3,716,213.10 |
| 13 | $ 11,350.52 | $ 416.67 | | $ - | $ - | $ (131,206.19) | $ 3,957,766.95 |
| 14 | $ 11,870.45 | $ 416.67 | | $ - | $ - | $ (137,445.44) | $ 4,215,021.81 |
| 15 | $ 12,406.78 | $ 416.67 | | $ - | $ - | $ (143,881.34) | $ 4,488,998.22 |

****Assets in the Dynamic Vault at the end of year 15 are utilized to fund Vault's 1,2,3 and Dynamic below for years 16 through 30.****

| | | Income Vault | | Vault 1[1] | Vault 2[2] | Vault 3[3] | Dynamic Vault[4] |
|---|---|---|---|---|---|---|---|
| | Allocation of Investment | | | 10.36% | 13.97% | 23.77% | 51.89% |
| | Annual Net Rate of Return* | | | 1.50% | 3.50% | 5.50% | 6.50% |
| Retirement Year | Monthly Income Required | VA w/5% Guaranteed Income[5] | | Years 1-3 | Years 4-7 | Years 8-15 | Years 15 + |
| Year 16 Beginning Balance | | $ 100,000.00 | | $465,168.46 | $627,110.66 | $1,067,245.35 | $ 2,329,473.75 |
| 16 | $ 12,960.00 | $ 416.67 | | $ (150,519.96) | $ 649,059.54 | $ 1,125,943.85 | $ 2,480,889.54 |
| 17 | $ 13,530.63 | $ 416.67 | | $ (157,367.58) | $ 671,776.62 | $ 1,187,870.76 | $ 2,642,147.36 |
| 18 | $ 14,119.22 | $ 416.67 | | $ (164,430.67) | $ 695,288.80 | $ 1,253,203.65 | $ 2,813,886.94 |
| 19 | $ 14,726.32 | $ 416.67 | | $ - | $ (171,715.89) | $ 1,322,129.85 | $ 2,996,789.59 |
| 20 | $ 15,352.51 | $ 416.67 | | $ - | $ (179,230.12) | $ 1,394,846.99 | $ 3,191,580.92 |
| 21 | $ 15,998.37 | $ 416.67 | | $ - | $ (186,980.43) | $ 1,471,563.58 | $ 3,399,033.67 |
| 22 | $ 16,664.51 | $ 416.67 | | $ - | $ (194,974.12) | $ 1,552,499.57 | $ 3,619,970.86 |
| 23 | $ 17,351.56 | $ 416.67 | | $ - | $ - | $ (203,218.70) | $ 3,855,268.97 |
| 24 | $ 18,060.16 | $ 416.67 | | $ - | $ - | $ (211,721.93) | $ 4,105,861.45 |
| 25 | $ 18,790.98 | $ 416.67 | | $ - | $ - | $ (220,491.78) | $ 4,372,742.45 |
| 26 | $ 19,544.71 | $ 416.67 | | $ - | $ - | $ (229,536.50) | $ 4,656,970.71 |
| 27 | $ 20,322.05 | $ 416.67 | | $ - | $ - | $ (238,864.56) | $ 4,959,673.80 |
| 28 | $ 21,123.72 | $ 416.67 | | $ - | $ - | $ (248,484.70) | $ 5,282,052.60 |
| 29 | $ 21,950.49 | $ 416.67 | | $ - | $ - | $ (258,405.92) | $ 5,625,386.02 |
| 30 | $ 22,803.13 | $ 416.67 | | $ - | $ - | $ (268,637.52) | $ 5,991,036.11 |

SUMMARY

| Original Investment | $ 3,003,176.58 |
|---|---|
| Received Investment Income (30 Years) | $ 4,873,889.18 |
| Remaining Balance | $ 6,091,036.11 |

This analysis will be based on the information and assumptions that you provided. You should not use it to obtain credit or for any purposes other than financial planning. Any tax aspects presented are for illustration only, and are based on current federal tax law and assumed tax rates.

Depicted rates of return are hypothetical and are not representative of the actual rate of return that you will experience with any particular insurance or financial product. Actual results will vary depending on the insurance or financial product you purchase, the amount of premiums or payments you make, the benefits, charges, expenses, guaranteed (if any) and non-guaranteed elements of the policy or product, and general market conditions. Asset allocation does not ensure a profit or protect against losses in a declining market.   Investments offering the potential for higher rates of return also involve a higher degree of risk.  Actual results will vary.

IMPORTANT: The illustration or other information generated by this analysis regarding the likelihood of various investment outcomes are hypothetical in nature, do not reflect actual investment results and are not guarantees of future results.

* Annual Net Rate of Return is net of all advisory fees and account expenses.  Hypothetical annual return averages are based off of the below indexes 10 year averages.

[1] Hypothetical Rate of Return for Vault 1  is based on 50% avg. of the 3 year Certificate of Deposit and 50% Barclays U.S. Agg. Bond Index

[2] Hypothetical Rate of Return for Vault 2 is based on 30%  S&P 500 Index and 50% Barclays U.S. Agg. Bond Index and 20% CDs

[3] Hypothetical Rate of Returnfor Vault 3 is  based on 60%  S&P 500 Index and 40% Barclays U.S. Agg. Bond Index

[4] Hypothetical Rate of Return for Vault 4 is based on 70%  S&P 500 Index, 20% Barclays U.S. Agg. Bond Index and 10% NAREIT Index

[5]Variable Annuity Guarantees are subject to the claims-paying ability of the issuing insurance company.  (See page 4 for additional disclosures)

**Bank CDs** are insured by the Federal Deposit Insurance Corporation and offer a fixed rate of return, whereas both the principal and yield of investment securities will fluctuate with changes in market conditions. Investments offering the potential for higher rates of return also involve a higher degree of risk.  Rates of return will vary over time, particularly for long-term investments.  Your actual

**Barclays U.S. Aggregate Bond Index** is an unmanaged index composed of the Barclays Government/Credit Bond Index, Mortgage-Backed Securities Index,

**S&P 500** is an index of 500 stocks chosen for market size, liquidity and industry grouping (among other factors), designed to be a leading indicator of U.S. equities and

**NAREIT Index** - An index that consists of all Real Estate Investment Trusts that currently trade on the New York Stock Exchange, the NASDAQ National Market System and the American Stock Exchange

Indices are unmanaged and do not incur fees or expenses. When applicable, these returns include the reinvestment of dividends. An investor cannot invest directly in an index.

## 😄 *Joke Time* 😄

## God's Time and Money

A preacher went into his church and he was praying to God. While he was praying, he asked God, "How long is 10 million years to you?" God replied, "1 second." The next day the preacher asked God, "God, how much is 10 million dollars to you?" And God replied, "A penny." Then finally the next day the preacher asked God, "God, can I have one of your pennies?" And God replied, "Just wait a sec."

* * *

The market may be bad, but I slept like a baby last night: I woke up every hour and cried.

* * *

The pessimist sees the glass as half empty. The optimist sees the glass half full. The financial advisor just adds whiskey.

# CHAPTER SIX

# I'm from the Government, and I'm Here to Help

**Y**OU'D BE HARD-PRESSED TO FIND A CLIENT WHO'S really looking forward to talking about this stuff. Heck, you'd probably have similar difficulties finding an advisor who puts it on the top of his list to do! Regardless of how intimidated you might be, and regardless of how worried you are about being bored to tears, you're doing yourself a disservice by not considering how Social Security, taxes, and healthcare are going to impact your retirement planning.

Working with a financial advisor who has relationships with CPAs and the proper legal and tax professionals may help ensure that you don't overlook any important changes in the labyrinth of codes and laws out there. Just like you would prepare by looking over your pension statements or 401k, you'll want to familiarize yourself with the rights and benefits you're entitled to as an

American citizen. After all, you've been paying into these systems your whole life. Don't you want to get something back?

## Social Security

We look at this piece of retirement planning as resting on a three-legged platform. The first and most important leg is Social Security.

When we talk about Social Security with clients who are nearing retirement age, the first issue we typically tackle is deciding at what age those clients are going to take social security. There are two choices: Most people elect to begin taking payments at sixty-six, but some take an extension to seventy. If the client is married and their spouse is also entitled to Social Security, there is the additional question of whether that spouse will take half the payments entitled to them now instead of waiting for both partners in the couple to defer until they are seventy. While we don't want to jump the gun on dipping into any assets, we also don't want to look a gift horse in the mouth, either—who knows what the health of the Social Security system will be in the next few decades, after all!

That's just the tip of the iceberg. Social Security is a very confusing issue, even without taking into account all the recent changes in the laws. According to *Investment News Contributor* and *Social Security Retirement Benefits* author Mary Beth Franklin, Social Security is a bigger piece of the puzzle than most folks realize. In her book, which we consider our financial roadmap, she says:

The simple truth is this: Social Security is the single largest source of income for the majority of Americans sixty-five and older, representing half or more of total income for 53% of married couples and 74% of unmarried individuals, according to the Social Security Administration. For more affluent clients typically seen by financial advisers, an informed decision about how and when to claim Social Security benefits can mean thousands of extra retirement income dollars per year and tens of thousands of dollars over a lifetime. **For a married couple, the right Social Security claiming decisions could boost their joint lifetime income by $100,000 or more.**

That's hardly small potatoes! And the more our clients can get from Social Security, the less they eventually need to pull out of their assets, and thus, the longer those assets will last. So it's critical to know when to take Social Security and when it'll do the best for you. When we discuss our vaults system, we'll explain how Social Security factors into it, as well as Cost of Living Adjustments (COLAs) and other related items.

Overall, we aim to make it as easy as possible for our clients to understand what Social Security means for them, what their options are, and how we can help navigate those waters. Armed with Franklin's text and other resources, we'll go through the most common questions about Social Security, run the numbers, deliver them to our clients in plain English, and strategize from there.

We also encourage everyone, whether you end up utilizing our services or not, to visit the Social Security Administration's website at **www.ssa.gov** as soon as possible. Where you once would have gotten an annual statement in the mail, all of this information is accessible online. You can view FAQs, use their Retirement Benefits Estimator, and read up on all aspects of the system.

## Taxes

Tax planning[1] is an integral part of financial planning, and one that too many financial advisors overlook, mostly because they don't have the specialized knowledge that a comprehensive financial advisor does. Like Social Security, the benefits of a maximized tax strategy are important because they reverberate down the line—if you can save a couple hundred dollars in taxes, compounded over the years, you will have a lot more money to work with.

We hear a lot in the news about taxes—who should pay more, and who should pay less. The simple truth is that most working people probably pay too many taxes—and before you get all excited, I'm not talking about politics here, I'm just talking about simple mathematics hidden in some very complex language and laws. Because it's not a part of most people's day-to-day activities—everyone is busy making a living, taking care of their kids, and figuring out how they're going to deal with everyday expenses and events—most people are not focused on being as tax-efficient as they can be. And although they may employ CPAs to help them with their once-a-year tax filing, CPAs really aren't trained in tax planning, tax efficiency, or taking the long view of how taxes fold into a retirement planning strategy. Although all cases are different,

---

1 Neither Advanced Wealth Strategies Group, John Levee, nor DFPG provide tax or legal advice, as such advice can only be provided by a qualified tax or legal professional, who all investors should consult prior to making any investment decisions.

as a general rule of thumb it's safe to say that most people could employ certain strategies to save additional taxes.

As comprehensive financial advisors with access to professional tax advice, we help our clients implement advantageous strategies like using tax-deferred vehicles such as IRAs or annuities. Being comprehensive means that we touch on everything: tax planning, income planning, tax savings, and estate planning. And all of these factors have to work well together so that one doesn't muck up the strategic impact of the other. For example, if you've got a reasonably high income and well-funded investment accounts, in addition to a 401k or IRA, you will probably pay both income tax and capital gains taxes. In those situations, your savings strategies may conflict with your tax planning strategy, instead of working with them. Depending on a number of factors, a comprehensive firm could potentially find a solution that allows you to save income and accumulate more assets over the long run. And tax-deferred strategies are particularly important when you consider that, once you retire, your income is not going to be as high as it is during your working years, and therefore your tax rate will be lower.

Knowing that, does it really make sense to keep doing the same old thing year after year without really looking at taxes from a strategic perspective? I don't think so, and I'm willing to bet you don't, either.

## Healthcare

We've talked about the importance of healthcare before, but we're going to linger on it a little more—it's just *that* important. While Uncle Sam is able to provide some assistance for qualified retirees through the Medicaid and Medicare programs, this might not always be the case. Even now, there are many medical procedures that the federal government might not cover. Long-term care is a whole other hornet's nest that Medicare can't help you with. It's hard enough to deal with a healthcare setback while you're young and still working. Imagine the catastrophic impact of a healthcare-related event once you're retired and unable to count on that physical and financial resiliency you might have once enjoyed.

This is precisely what we do with our clients—we have them imagine the "What If" scenarios. What if you have to pay for your own healthcare? How long will your money last if you or your spouse needs long-term care? What if you and your spouse fall ill at the same time? These are real questions that you'll need real answers for if you hope to be protected both during and after a crisis—and certainly if you hope to shield your children and family members from the very real financial toll that long-term care issues take.

In that same spirit, while we do include Medicare benefits in our financial plan for our clients, we always encourage discussions and contingency plans for how they will deal with medical expenses in the face of diminished (or lack of) support from the Medicare system. Obviously, we don't know what the future of Medicare will be—we don't expect it to go anywhere, but we would be doing our clients a disservice if we didn't plan for a possible future in which it no longer benefitted us. My own father had a triple bypass and cataract surgery in both eyes before he passed away—all of which were covered by Medicare. As you know from earlier anecdotes, he died without any money to his name. He certainly wouldn't have been able to afford those surgeries without Medicare coverage, and we never would have let him suffer without undergoing those procedures. By failing to plan for all eventualities, you're not just talking about the ruin of your own finances—you're placing a pretty hefty burden on your children, too.

So what's to be done, other than making sure that you fully understand the benefits you're entitled to under Medicare? In the spirit of planning for the future, we'll discuss all of the big points in our initial meeting. And while we're not insurance peddlers by any means, we've got relationships with insurance brokers who can help our clients set up adequate long-term care coverage, enabling them to start retirement without that very real, very dark cloud of worry hanging over their heads.

A stockbroker says to his colleague: "I don't think this line of work is for you. You just keep losing money all the time."

"You're right," he replied. "My whole life, all I've done is lose money." Next day he comes to work and resigns. His coworker asks, "What are you going to do for living?"

"I finally figured out how I can make some money from losing money all the time."

"How?"

"I am going to build a web page and take it public!"

* * *

One day at a local café, a woman suddenly called out, "My daughter's choking! She swallowed a nickel! Please, anyone, help!"

Immediately a man at a nearby table rushed up to her and said he was experienced in these situations. He calmly stepped over to the girl, then with no look of concern, wrapped his arms around her and squeezed. Out popped the nickel.

The man returned to his table as if nothing had happened.

"Thank you!" the mother cried. "Tell me, are you a doctor?"

"No," the man replied. "I work for the IRS."

# CHAPTER SEVEN

# Keeping Money from Ruining Your Family

**N**O ONE LIKES TO TALK ABOUT ESTATE PLANNING—NOT even people who get paid to talk about it, really. And why is that? Let's face facts here: when we talk about estate planning, we're talking about dying. There's no sense in sugarcoating it. I tell this to all of my clients: "***Ain't none of us getting out of here alive.***"

Over the years, I've come to swear by the beauty of this blunt approach. Call it gallows humor, call it ripping off the Band-Aid; whatever you call it, it works. Once we've dealt with that uncomfortable and cringe-worthy truth about estate planning, there's really nothing else to be afraid of, and so, there's no reason to keep putting it off! In that spirit, let's dive in. Hopefully, you'll come out on the other side better equipped to deal with any and all eventualities.

## Basic Estate Planning: What's Involved?

Ultimately, having an estate plan is about making sure you do the best you possibly can in your lifetime by making arrangements to leave a financial legacy. I practice what I preach – my wife and I are, even now, in the process of revisiting our documents to make sure everything is shipshape and in its right place. We want to be able to preserve some wealth to pass on to our children, and to make sure that wealth isn't squandered. We know that our children might not have the same opportunities that we've had, and we can't be sure what the economy will do over the course of the next forty years.

After planning to make our own retirement as happy and secure as possible, we want to make sure that we pass any remaining wealth on to our kids and chosen charities in the most tax efficient and foolproof manner we possibly can. With all things in estate planning, I like to say that you pray for the best, but you plan for the worst.

At its heart, estate planning begins with the basic documents: a will or living trust, for example. Personally, I prefer a well-written living trust, because it is in effect while you are alive and can easily be amended as life changes. My wife and I have often made minor changes to our trust before heading for the airport. The trust can also be used to manage assets "from the grave."

Now, what do I mean by that? You may have a child that cannot manage money (it's amazing how many families have this issue). That is a situation you can plan for, including instructions for asset management and distribution. But worse than a child with no head for money are kids who don't get along. One or more may be greedy or have a controlling spouse. One may suffer from the old "Mom and Dad liked you best" syndrome and want to get even, even if it costs them or the estate money.

Parents like to think that this could never happen, not to their children, but believe me, it happens. It happened within our family. It happened in my wife's family. It could happen in yours. Through the years we have seen many of these situations occur. It tears a family apart, sometimes beyond repair. It pits siblings against siblings.

I recall one situation that almost takes the cake. Several years ago a particular client passed away. This person had been a client for many years and we had a great relationship. Not only had we enjoyed a healthy, fruitful client/advisor relationship, but we had become good friends. This happens frequently in our practice – some of our clients have been with us over twenty years. This client's children did not get along. To make it even worse, the client had been helping to support them for years. (*This happens more than you may realize.*)

When my client found out that the end was coming fairly quickly, we had a meeting during which she divulged her greatest fear. No, it was not the fact that she was dying and the end was near, even though we both had a pretty good cry as we talked about her impending death. It was much worse. She was positive her children were going to fight over the assets. I tried to dispel that notion, telling her, "My goodness! Why would they fight when each will inherit over a half million in assets? That makes no sense whatsoever." I was wrong. The war they fought over her estate was vicious, despite promising my client before she died that they intended to respect the trust. So much for promises. I tried to intervene and in so doing, almost put myself and my company in jeopardy. When attorneys get involved in estate planning, two things typically happen. I call it the extending cross. Settlement expenses go up, sometimes dramatically, and settlement time stretches out. Sometimes it takes years for the estate to settle. The case I'm highlighting here may still not be settled. Remember, there's not a whole lot of incentive for the attorneys to wrap it up.

I wish that client had given everything to charity, or completed a bucket list. (Even I think I could handle Skydiving or 3.7 seconds on a wild bull! Anything but giving it to unappreciative, leeching kids who hate each other!)

There are thousands of nightmare stories out there, and there is no perfect solution. No silver bullet. No hero to the rescue. One thing that can be done is to implement a total estate plan that includes a Living Trust with explicit detailed instructions for the Successor Trustee(s) to follow. Liquidating illiquid assets like real estate can also help. Cash, stock accounts, mutual fund accounts and many other assets can be easily divided upon our deaths, and the values are indisputable. *Remember* – none of us are getting out of here alive. These are the tough conversations we must have with our clients. Husband and wives, fathers and mothers must have these serious important conversations. Leave as little to chance as humanly possible. Remember, we are available to help. Just give us a call. This is too big a potential problem to not talk to someone very experienced in this area.

Although there is no way for us to have "seen it all," we have seen enough to help you make the right kinds of decisions, relating to all different types of estate plans. We try to guide you to the right people, and give you our professional opinions. Remember: whether working with us or anybody else, the right questions are always a necessity.

A good estate plan covers much more than just that. There are many ancillary documents—right to die paperwork, powers of attorney (including healthcare and financial), advanced medical directives, long-term care instructions—that need to be addressed in the estate planning package as well.

We have included a basic checklist for your convenience. It is a good place to start—something to get you off the fence, something to hopefully make you do something to prepare for the inevitable. We go deeper than this with our clients and you should be sure that you do the same, but for now, take a look:

## Estate Planning Checklist

❑ **Communicating your Wishes:**

   ❑ Do you have a current and valid will?

   ❑ If you have a will, have you reviewed it within the last 3 years?

   ❑ Have you named executor(s) and trustee(s)?

   ❑ Do you have an enduring power of attorney?

   ❑ Have you made a nomination in relation to your superannuation?

- ❑ If you have specific wishes regarding your funeral, have you left instructions with your executor?

- ❑ Have you documented your wishes regarding organ donations?

## ❑ Protecting your Family:

- ❑ Does your spouse/children/executor know the names and addresses of your professional advisers?

- ❑ Does your will name a guardian(s) for minor children?

- ❑ Does your will provide for children from a previous marriage(s)?

- ❑ If you have dependents with disabilities does your estate plan protect their interests?

- ❑ Do you have the right amount and type of life insurance?

## ❑ Protecting their inheritance:

- ❑ Have you considered setting up a trust to protect your family's inheritances?

- ❑ Does your estate plan take account of the possibility of someone making a claim on your estate?

- ❑ Does your will protect potential beneficiaries who may face family breakdown or become bankrupt?

- ❑ Do you know what effect your death would have on your self-managed super fund, family trust or family company?

## ❑ Other Considerations:

- ❑ Have you considered making a planned gift to charity?

- ❑ Do you know what the tax and social security consequences would be for beneficiaries of your current will?

## Planning for Your Business

Apart from financial cushions for medical necessities not covered by Medicare, including long-term care insurance, if you own a business—even in your retirement—that business needs to be included as an asset to be protected and managed in your estate plan. This includes properly insuring against liability by structuring the business properly—such as an LLC or S-Corp or C-Corp, for instance—as opposed to a sole proprietorship, which will thus separate your individual liability and assets from the liabilities of the business. As Mark Twain so wisely told us: "It's not what you make; it's what you keep." Including a business in your estate plans also includes devising an inheritance plan for the shares of the business, or you must have a clear, concise business continuation plan and document in place, whether it's divided among business partners, children, or both. Once again, there are innumerable nightmare stories about business owners dying while the remaining spouse ends up empty handed. Don't let it happen to you!

## Planning for Charitable Legacy Giving

A thorough estate planning conversation will include charitable giving, if that's something that makes sense for you and is important to you and/or your spouse. Many people fall into the trap of thinking that if they don't have children, they don't need to make a thorough effort to take care of estate arrangements for third parties. If your church or a charity is important to you, trust me, you do not want a probate court making these decisions if you fail to properly execute an estate plan. To ensure that your wishes are followed to the letter, a comprehensive financial advisor working with an attorney can structure charitable trusts, annuities, and other vehicles to help you fund the causes and churches you cherish the most. If you do have children, these same professionals can assist in advising you on how to divide your assets between those children and the charities.

## What Happens If I Don't Have A Proper Estate Plan?

The short answer: nothing good, friends! If you fail to have a properly executed will, most states will designate you as having died intestate. This means, essentially, that the state has a will for you and a plan for your money, and I'm willing to bet it's not even remotely close to what you had in mind for your financial legacy. On top of that, states vary in what arbitrary fees they charge to settle these cases in probate court. If you don't have a proper estate plan in place and your assets end up in probate, and there is any contestation of the will, the lawyers are going to be the ones who end up winning big while your heirs duke it out on the sidelines, on the losing end of the fight.

This is the kind of thing we and our clients work very hard to avoid. By having a proper estate plan, you can typically take these decisions out of the hands of the courts. There is a myriad of ways to arrange an estate plan that fits the particulars of your situation—living trusts, wealth transfer trusts, IRA conduit trusts, handicapped children trusts, revocable living trusts, etc.—and all you have to do is find someone willing to really sit down and go through your needs with you.

Often, individuals will head straight for an attorney's office to settle these matters. That's certainly a sensible solution, and better than doing nothing at all, but we advocate that clients work with a team consisting of at least a financial advisor and an attorney to structure the estate plan. A certified public accountant (CPA) may be a good addition to the team as well, depending on the size of the estate and whether or not pre- tax dollars make up a large portion of the estate. The reason for this is that financial advisors are attuned to consequences in a different way than the attorney—first, if they have worked closely and comprehensively with your family over the years, they know the true nuts and bolts of your estate. That advisor has a sense of your liabilities and your assets, your concerns, and your family's financial dynamic in a way that most attorneys won't. It's simply not part of the equation for them. As a comprehensive financial advisor who meets with most clients at least once per quarter, I'm able to understand a client's life in ways that an attorney generally won't be able to in just a meeting or two. Additionally, many people need a trust instead of a simple reciprocating wills.

By the same token, not all financial advisors are created equal. Either through lack of training or lack of time (such as advisors who depend on commissions to stay in business, rather than on collecting fees for their work), they might not be prepared to walk you through all the facets of your estate plan. When you're interviewing a financial advisor, make sure to get a feel for how much training they've had around the subject. How important is estate planning to them? How much experience have they had in dealing with estate planning? It's crucial to ask these questions up front, rather than assuming that you're dealing with someone who has the experience that you're looking for. Remember: no one cares more about your money than you do, so make sure you care about it a great deal.

## What If I Have a Child Who Can't Manage Money? (Or Children Who Can't Manage to Get Along?)

In over a quarter century of experience with this subject, I've found that maybe one out of every three families I deal with has at least one child who just can't seem to manage money well. While this will certainly cause more than its fair share of headaches while you are alive, if this is your situation, you're not going to be able to spend your retirement years feeling very good about what's going to happen after you're gone. In these cases, the only way to deal with a child who can't manage money, if you truly care about them and want them to live a reasonable life with the money they're going to inherit, is to make a plan *for* them.

Having a proper estate plan means that you can manage this money for those aforementioned trouble children from the *grave*. But the key here is that you've got to make those plans *before* you get there! Be it through a will with a testamentary trust, a revocable living trust, or some other properly executed method, there are ways to control the flow of money into each child's bank account. This can only be accomplished with comprehensive trust planning.

Additionally, you may want to consider a corporate trustee. What is a corporate trustee? It is a professional firm that specializes in trust management. A firm that is properly licensed and bonded to provide these necessary services. And let me be very emphatic with this statement. *I AM NOT TALKING ABOUT A BANK TRUST DEPARTMENT!* In my experience and opinion, a bank trust department is the last corporate trustee I would ever recommend to my clients. There are *so many* reasons to avoid banks as corporate Trustees.

My biggest beef with banks as corporate trustees relates to fees and what I think may be conflicts of interest. We use a couple of true corporate Trustees. These firms do not offer investments (that's my job), they do not know the family dynamics (that too is my job). These firms simply follow the mandates of the trust to the letter, which is important because it helps to eliminate most of a family's Hatfields/McCoys potential. I love my family dearly and the last thing I want to see grow in my family is greed, division, or a feeling of being cheated. I have seen far too much of that in my career. That's the very last thing I would ever want to happen to the people I've spent my life loving and protecting.

My fantastic wife, Laurie, and I have worked very hard for many years and have been blessed beyond our wildest dreams. We have four very intelligent and capable sons. There is no way I would want to burden any of them with successor trusteeship. They, like most everyone else, are busy with jobs, children, and everything else that makes up their life. Why add additional burden and stress by making them deal with the settlement of a trust, or pit them against one another? Not on my watch! I don't want any animosity, jealousy, or feeling that favoritism is being employed. That's why we have a corporate trustee designated for duty after Laurie and I are gone. I'll bet many of you feel the same way.

If you are currently working with a comprehensive financial advisor, they should already be familiar with the issues you might face regarding a child who has no money management skills, and can steer you towards a properly drawn and executed estate plan. This is especially important for the very wealthy client who now may be able to pass on millions—free of estate taxes, if done properly—we're not talking small potatoes. Sophisticated estate planning also makes provisions for changes in future estate tax law structures.

Another common problem that crops up in families with more than one heir is that the family dynamics can often end up dragging estate plans back into court in an attempt to rip them to shreds. Here again, the attorneys rake in the money while the family falls to pieces. We've had clients pass away and leave estates to siblings who absolutely hated each other, and used the process of contesting the will as just another excuse to have a knock- down, drag out fight. Because we've been there since the beginning, we knew the whole story, and were able to navigate it better than a stranger would— mostly because we started navigating the situation long before it even *became* a situation. We knew that this would be an issue, so we safeguarded the client's wishes by making an airtight estate plan.

Even in families where the children get along just fine, it's foolish to think that will always be the case. I've seen money do wonderful things for people throughout my life, but I've also seen it do awful things to people, and that includes families. "My kids get along just fine," a client will tell us. "We don't have to worry about that." It's only true until you're gone and the money has to be dealt with—and then animosity becomes a very real, very tangible possibility. If a properly structured estate plan does get contested, the plaintiff isn't going to have much of a leg to stand on, and years of heartache and animosity can be nipped in the bud. If you care about the health of your family long past when you'll be here to watch over them, taking the time to invest in your estate plan is one surefire way to show that.

## 😄 *Joke Time* 😄

A young banker decided to get his first tailor-made suit. As he tried it on, he reached down to put his hands in the pockets but to his surprise found none.

He mentioned this to the tailor who asked him, "You're a banker, right?"

The young man answered, "Yes, I am."

"Well, whoever heard of a banker putting his hand in his own pocket?"

* * *

Bankers are people that help you with problems you would not have had without them.

* * *

Hospitals report that the hearts of bankers are in strong demand by transplant patients, because they've never been used.

* * *

A businessman was confused about a bill he had received, so he asked his secretary for some mathematical help.

"If I were to give you $20,000, minus 14%, how much would you take off?" he asked her.

The secretary replied, "Everything but my earrings."

# The Rest of Your Life

FINANCIAL AND ESTATE PLANNING CAN BE OVER-whelming, especially when done by amateurs and poorly trained advisors with little experience, but that doesn't mean it's impossible by any means. If done correctly, and with the help of a trusted professional, we think it can even be a little fun—and here's why. When you're making a financial plan, you're opening yourselves up to a wonderful world of *possibility*. You've worked hard your entire life, and now you're taking the steps to make sure that you can enjoy the fruits of that labor. You're making sure that your family will be taken care of in the years to come, even when you're not there to watch them grow. And, not to be too smug about it, when people who haven't put in the time to plan are fussing and fretting, you'll hopefully be enjoying a certain kind of freedom. Once their plans are in place, my clients find that the biggest benefit to them is the *peace of mind* of actually having a plan. You can have it too! Don't procrastinate another day.

In order to have a truly diversified portfolio, you need to work with a financial advisor who can take you outside of the emotional zone in which individual investors operate. Too often, individual investors have prejudices or unrealistic expectations about the markets. This isn't surprising; I bet you know a lot more than I do about your profession, for instance, and financial advising is no different. At our firm, we have access to research that the individual investor doesn't. We have access to information that the individual investor doesn't. And most important: we have access to the objectivity that an individual investor doesn't. We're able to see the big picture, if you're willing to put in the work to look honestly at your expenses, your expectations, and your estate plans.

While we know you might not end up working with us—maybe this guide was all you needed to get started, or maybe you have a professional who knows your family and who you're already comfortable with—as stewards of our profession, we want to encourage you to take the information you've learned here and apply it to your present and future dealings with your financial advisor. We want you to be able to go out armed with the right questions to ask, and a sense of what the right answers are.

For your convenience, here's a simple checklist of things to look for in a financial planner.

1. **Does the planner work as part of a team?** (No one person can be constantly at work. A good planner has a team of qualified, experienced professionals backing him up and making sure that no part of your financial plan slips through the cracks.)

2. **Does the planner have a plan for a bear market?** (A good planner knows he can't just bury his head in the sand until the danger has passed. He must be prepared and ready to help you when things go wrong.)

3. **Does the planner rely on an old-fashioned buy-and-hold strategy?** (A good planner is up to date on the latest economic theories and keeps himself aware of industry innovations.)

4. **Does the planner have experience working with investment opportunities that aren't stocks and bonds?** (A good planner will understand that diversifying your portfolio also means looking outside the stock market for investment opportunities.)

5. **Does the planner recognize the importance of budgeting?** (A good planner recognizes that life on a fixed income carries its own challenges and will work with you to build a budget you can realistically use.)

6. **Is the planner willing to meet with you frequently?** (Quarterly meetings ensure that all parties are kept up to date on family changes and changes in the markets.)

7. **How many years of experience is the planner drawing on?** (A good planning team's collective experience should be measured in decades.)

8. **What independent research team does the planner consult?** (A good planner should work with at least one dedicated research team.)

Unfortunately, in our profession, all practitioners are not created equal. There are fantastically knowledgeable, experienced, caring advisors who are absolutely dedicated to taking care of their clients. Thankfully, we believe our firm falls into that category. Unfortunately, there are others that don't fit that category. And of course there are the crooks—you will find them in every field. Ours is no different. The same goes for doctors, lawyers, CPAs, engineers, architects … you get the picture. Thank God there are enough honest and caring ones. ***Make sure you are working with one of them!***

In the meantime, we're always here if you want to send those questions our way at **www.advancegroup.biz,** or **www. animascapital.com.**

9 781947 368330